STICKS
and
STONES

By Sandra D. Alexander

Trilogy Christian Publishers

A Wholly Owned Subsidary of Trinity Broadcasting Network

2442 Michelle Drive

Tustin, CA 92780

Title: Sticks and Stones

For information, address Trilogy Christian Publishing

Rights Department, 2442 Michelle Drive, Tustin, Ca 92780.

Trilogy Christian Publishing/ TBN and colophon are trademarks of Trinity Broadcasting Network.

For information about special discounts for bulk purchases, please contact Trilogy Christian Publishing.

Manufactured in the United States of America

10 9 8 7 6 5 4 3 2 1

Library of Congress Cataloging-in-Publication Data is available.

ISBN 979-8-88738-210-4

ISBN 979-8-88738-211-1 (ebook)

In loving memory of "Charlie."
March 04, 1974 – October 04, 2018

Your love and thirst for life gave me the courage and strength to leave a very toxic marriage. I pray that my journey moving forward makes you proud.

Love you forever and always.

xoxoxoxo

My Gratitude

To my family and friends,

I would not have had the strength, let alone the courage, to make such bold moves that ultimately allowed the possibility of a healthy life for me and the kids without you. Some knew from the beginning the extent of the manipulative abuse, while others only had a glimpse into my world. Regardless, my community kept my flame of hope from being extinguished completely, and I thank you from the bottom of my heart!

God, thank you for hitting me over the head with that proverbial rolling pin and shining a brilliant light! You have become the center of my life and define who I am.

CONTENTS

FOREWORD

"Sticks and Stones may break my bones, but words will never hurt me."

This rhyme is meant to be empowering. If only it were true. Words can and do hurt. As a Licensed Professional Counselor, I am reminded of that fact nearly every working day of my life.

If you've experienced the pain and trauma of hurtful words in your marriage, you will easily identify with the author of this book.

Sandra's account will remind you that relationships are complex, that the people we know in public may be entirely different people at home, and that questions such as, "Why doesn't she just leave?" serve only to further isolate a person who desperately needs support, understanding, and resources.

Ultimately, *Sticks and Stones* is a story of faith in God and commitment to integrity, values, and morals in the face of devastating abuse.

I found Sandra's account to be like a life well lived—full of pain, but also inspiring and redemptive. I'm confident that you will find it to be the same.

Isaac Dunning, LPC

(Pseudonym to protect the identity of the author.)

PREFACE

This is a true story. The characters in this book are real. Names have been changed and locations altered to protect the innocent. To emphasize the magnitude of the verbal manipulation and hatred experienced, the texts and emails used are told exactly as they occurred.

PRAYER

July 2018

Dear Lord Jesus,

My heart is filled with joy and enthusiasm. I can't thank you enough for being with me every step of the way. My prayers are a broad spectrum, like that of a rainbow, wanting to touch every soul.

For my husband—

Dear Lord ... May he truly know you. May he find peace, comfort, and joy in You. His life is filled with fear and hatred. I have honestly forgotten why I fell in love with him. That sense of completeness is no longer. Dear Lord, I can't make my husband happy ... that is between You and him. My marriage to this man is broken and only You can fix it, if that is Your will. I trust in you, Lord. I give this burden to you. Please Lord, heal this broken heart.

In your amazing name ... Amen

INTRODUCTION

2018 brought with it tears and shattered hearts, however, it also brought with it courage, strength, and a true appreciation that we are NEVER alone.

I lost my 44-year-old brother to cancer. His thirst, his fight for life, opened my eyes and my heart to a very difficult decision I had to make. I was terrified!

When Charlie first told me that he had cancer, I remember breaking down in tears. My tears were not just for my brother; I also cried because I knew I would not get the support from my husband to go and spend time with him. I knew deep down I would have to fight every step of the way. That fight became a battle; it became too real.

The summer of 2018 was one of trying to reinsert a part of me that had been pushed aside— suppressed for years. You see, over the years, I had to adjust my personality to accommodate my husband's wants and needs. The act of walking on eggshells unfortunately became a norm, and slowly but surely, our "happy" was far from healthy. Our "happy" was conditional on whether or not it was acceptable to my husband.

Many people who are victims of abuse live in homes or environments where they become so accustomed to the situation, they consider it normal. They do not even see it is abuse because there is no physical injury; instead, there is an ongoing emotional barrage, which can be just as damaging. The scars are REAL!

August 02, 2018 was when that proverbial "straw that broke the camel's back" took place. My story, *Sticks and Stones*, unveils many of the details of what led up to this. However, it was when my husband accused me of lying about my brother's cancer just so I could take a trip to California—my hands are even trembling as I type these words—there was no love; there was no trust; there was no empathy—our marriage was based on fear and control. It was time.

Later that month, the children and I left. We left a home and a life that we tried for years to make happy and healthy. We left in the middle of the night with very little— with a duffle bag and $5.00.

Happily ever after? Unfortunately, not yet. My dear baby brother lost his battle with cancer. If there is a silver lining, I fought to spend time with Charlie and his beautiful family, and we have some amazing memories to cherish. Charlie gave me the strength and courage to step out of a toxic existence. Friends and family came out of the woodwork to encourage and help us and— yes, there is an AND— there were smiles on my children's faces. Just knowing that there are endless possibilities, my heart is healing.

We are meant to thrive, not simply survive. I have always been a dreamer, a very optimistic soul. When I started to see that part of me get snuffed out by someone else's fear and control, which was supposedly love and protection, my heart was screaming that something had to change.

I am not writing these words to trash my husband or air our dirty laundry; rather, I am sharing a very small part of my life in hopes that I can help just one person who might be trapped and terrified the way I was.

Was it easy? Absolutely not! Was it worth it? YES!

God continues to challenge my faith as another loved one is faced with cancer and I am in the throes of untying the knot after twenty-two years and trying to find a career at age fifty-seven to support my family. BUT these are only a few bumps in my road ahead. We can actually live again. We have HOPE! We can DREAM without the threat of someone else discrediting those dreams and tearing them apart.

In 2018, I lost my brother, but gained his spirit! In 2018, I left my house, but found my heart and home with ones who truly care.

"God bless us, everyone!" - Tiny Tim.

DREAMS

What are dreams? Who and where do they come from? Do they have tangible meaning or are they just an accumulation of thoughts throughout one's life that come to life in some form or another while we sleep?

This question is quite profound, and I believe many people have asked the very same question.

I rarely thought about my dreams. If they were nice, I would wake up delighted that the movie that had just played in my head was happy. If, on the other hand, the dreams were nightmares, well, then I would try to dismiss the experience, shake it off, and get on with my day.

As I have gotten older, I have, however, had dreams that have made me pause and stop to think. These are the ones that have stayed with me. Every detail is imprinted in my brain and on my heart. They are the visions that I did not "think up," but rather were introduced to me while I was asleep. It was as if I was invited onto the set of a movie. I was as much a player in it as I was a witness or a member of the audience.

In 2013, I had three dreams. These encounters came

months apart from one another. Each had its own tone, and each made a significant impact on my waking life. In 2013, God was preparing me for a very difficult season that I would need to walk through in order for my children and myself to be safe. The dreams which I am about to share came years before our escape. I truly believe that without these visions, I would not have had the strength to do what needed to be done.

Blanket of Snow:

As I drifted off to sleep into this dream, I awoke within at the top of a mountain. It was a landscape of deep, soft, fluffy snow. It was warm, as if I was wrapped up in this pure white blanket. I was, however, quite confused, because I do not ski, nor am I familiar with a scene like this. In this encounter, I was reaching out to help people who were getting off a ski lift. There was no fear of falling, because what I believed to be the hand of Jesus was steadying me from behind. There was no time equated to this happening. It could have been minutes, days, or even years. There was an overwhelming sense of peace and joy.

Within the same dream, the outdoor scene transitioned to indoors. I was sitting, no, rather leaning at the foot of Jesus. I didn't see His face, but I knew it was Him. We were in this amazing banquet hall. The room was dimly lit, ornately decorated, warm, and very welcoming. The foods presented on the table were none less than a gourmet feast. I was in awe of the presentation. I felt like a little girl walking into a room that offered everything she had ever dreamt of. I heard His voice encouraging me to enjoy, to eat whatever I wanted to, but I was already completely satisfied. My response as I leaned into His robe was, "Thank you, but I am satiated; I am complete." I closed my eyes, enjoying the fullness of being with our Lord.

When I woke, I felt a safety, a completeness that I had never felt before. I so wanted to go back to sleep and return to this space and time, but my waking reality called for my attention. Almost ten years later, I can still feel the essence of being in such a beautiful place.

> *And I pray that you, being rooted and established in love, may have power, together with all the Lord's people, to grasp how wide and how long and high and deep is the love of Christ, and to know this love that surpasses knowledge – that you may be filled to the measure of all the fullness of God.*
>
> **Ephesians 3:17-19 (NIV)**

Dance on Ice:

This dream was brief but ever so impactful. To give my readers a reference, I had always dreamt of being a figure skater as a little girl. The elegance and effortlessness of these athletes always intrigued me, and I could only imagine how it felt to fly with ease on the ice.

I do not remember the exact date, but I can close my eyes today and transport myself back into that place. It was an indoor ice rink. It was dark except for a spotlight shining on the ice. The stands where an audience would be sitting were empty and in the shadows. I was on the ice, but I wasn't. It was strange because I knew that I was present. I was struggling in my attempt to skate. Out of nowhere, a gentleman appeared. He was dressed in gray and came over to me. He spoke to me without speaking. He told me to stop trying, only to lean on him. Sighing, I let go of my struggle and leaned into his arms. As I did, we began a dance on ice that was beyond magical. It was effortless and flawless! I did not want this moment to end.

When I did wake up, the words that kept repeating in my mind were, STOP TRYING. It struck me that the gray figure must have been the Holy Spirit. I have been unequally yoked, and I needed to "let go and let God."

Then Jesus said, "Come to me, all of you who are weary and carry heavy burdens, and I will give you rest. Take my yoke upon you. Let me teach you, because I am humble and gentle at heart, and you will find rest for your souls. For my yoke is easy to bear, and the burden I give you is light."

Matthew 11:28-30 (NLT)

Fire - Engulfed in Flames:

Dramatic, intense, terrifying, heart-stopping—this event was so much more than a simple nightmare. On this evening, my heart literally stopped, and I watched myself from above as my body was being consumed by flames! It was dark. I was pleading with a being, and my words were being overshadowed by—something I can't even describe. I was being pulled into a void and all I can remember saying was a repetition of "Praise Jesus, Praise Jesus, Praise Jesus!" My body was being sucked down into flames! I was now out of my body and looking down at myself in the bed. I wasn't breathing; my heart had stopped.

Then, all at once, all at the same exact moment, my dog, a 68-pound Golden Retriever, jumped on my chest. The hand of God came swooping in to lift me out of this horrific place. I was back in my body. Gasping for breath, I woke up!

God was most definitely at the helm! As I sat up, all these dreams came flooding back into my memory. Every single detail connected with every single emotion. I knew without a doubt that He was preparing me for something very difficult. The sequence of the dreams is incredibly significant as well, because knowing who I am, if God revealed to me the hell I would need to go through before sharing with me what the result would most likely be, I honestly believe my children and I would still be trapped in a very toxic situation.

"And God will exalt you in due time, if you humble yourselves under his mighty hand" (1 Peter 5:6).

God is good, and His plans are perfect!

Run, but You Can't Hide

Dear Lord, show me where to begin. How do I even recall this time in my life? It was dark. It was terrifying. It was tragically REAL! I was fragile and scared, but You gave me the courage and the strength to make it through. You prepared me for a season which I could not have wished on anyone! I was emptied out of all options. You paved a way.

2018 -

I would love to start this story with "the day started as any other ordinary day," however, for my children and me, our ordinary was not typical of a healthy family. Our ordinary was dictated by the emotional composition (composure) of a narcissist.

On August 19, 2018, I was cleaning the house in preparation for my nephew's arrival. Tyler is my sister, Grace's

22-year-old son. Over the years, Ty had visited with us in Ketchikan, Alaska. He would come up to enjoy what the remoteness of the last frontier could offer—fishing, hunting, hiking, and the likes. This visit, however, was going to be different. This visit was going to open and expose a wound that had been festering for years.

I was going about my day as normal—cleaning, shopping, and cooking. Tyler's flight was scheduled to arrive at Ketchikan's International Airport around 7:00 pm. I had asked my husband, Ronald, if he wouldn't mind picking Ty up so that I could continue cleaning and getting dinner ready and have it on the table when he arrived. In fact, when Ron said he would think about it, I remember encouraging him to go.

"Come on, it'll be good for you to get out. The weather is beautiful, and you can pick him up in the Little Red Mustang. It'll be fun for you both."

The day was getting on, and Ron still had not given me a definite answer as to whether he would pick Tyler up. At this point, I was only to assume he would not and that I would have to run to the airport. This did not necessarily irritate me, because it was typical. When Ron asked me to do something for him, 99% of the time, I would. On the other hand, when I asked my husband to do something for me, he would always make some snide remark as to why it didn't concern him, so why should he bother!

It was now around 5:30 p.m. The airport was a very quick fifteen-minute ride from the house. Ketchikan is located on an island in the Southeast region of Alaska. It is a very beautiful community, however quite remote, and although Revillagigedo Island is large, Ketchikan has only thirty miles of road.

I asked my husband once again if he would please go to the airport for me. He declined. He decided it was time to pour himself a drink, watch the news, and grumble at the world.

The house was clean, the table was set, and the dinner was pretty much prepared. I just needed to put the spanakopita in the oven once we got home. I asked both the kids if they wanted to ride with me. Noah politely declined, but our daughter, Sophia, said that she would love to go if we could first stop at the local coffee shop.

"Of course, sweetie! Get ready, so we can head out," I responded.

"Emma said that she wanted to come too. Can we pick her up on the way?" Sophie asked.

"I don't see why not. Does Miss Jean know?" I inquired.

"Think so," Sophie replied.

"Well, I'll text her to be sure. Come on, let's go," I said while encouraging my daughter out the door.

Emma was Sophie's best friend. She and her mom, Jean, lived just down the street in the direction of the airport. The girls had spent a lot of time together. In fact, Jean has been a wonderful friend whom I have really been able to talk to. She was in an abusive marriage and finally found the strength to say, "enough is enough." She got out after seventeen years.

Sophie and I left the house just after 6:00 p.m. We stopped by Jean's house to pick up Em. Jean was home, and we chatted for a bit. She was quite concerned. We were discussing the details of a plan my sister and I had come up with on how I would get the children and myself out of Ketchikan without Ronald knowing. Months, if not years prior to this day, the situation at home was no longer healthy; in fact, it was toxic and fringing on dangerous. Ronald was becoming more and more controlling. In his mind, his way was the only way. Family coming up to Alaska for a visit was fine, but for the children and me to travel to the lower 48…well, his reaction would be so extreme, it was beyond intense. He would glare at me with dead, cold eyes. The hatred behind his glare would be tangible. There was no soul, as if the person that I knew was gone.

He would ALWAYS start with the reasoning that we had no money to spare. If that didn't work, then he would equate the lower 48 with living in a war zone. From there, he would most certainly speak ill of my family, accusing them of—where do I even begin! And when I say "reasoning," what I mean by that is "lecturing." There was never a conversation. It was always one-sided.

This is just a glimpse of why the children and I desperately needed to leave.

The plan, however, was one that was concerning not only to my friend, Jean, but, as it turned out, was worrisome to many others.

I will back up and fill in some gaps. In March of 2018, my younger brother was diagnosed with cancer. We did not know the extent of the cancer at first, but what I did know was that I wanted and needed to spend some time with him. I wanted to be there to help out as much as possible. I also knew that my husband would NEVER support my decision to go. He would make life a living, breathing nightmare, as if living in purgatory. From the silent treatments, lectures, insults, to threats of divorce and remarrying (like he can just go to the grocery store and pick out a new wife!). Yes, any decision without his 100% approval made our lives behind closed doors beyond difficult.

My brother Charlie, his beautiful wife, Andrea, and their sweet little girl, Lynn, lived in San Francisco, California.

From the time Charlie was diagnosed with cancer in March until the fateful day of August 19, I found the courage and the strength to go to California TWICE. I purposely emphasize the word twice, because Ron knew how to twist the facts. To gain sympathy from friends and family, he painted a picture as though I were flying back and forth between Alaska and California on a weekly basis, taking out a second mortgage on our house in the process.

The first trip was March 31 through April 11. The timing was such that it was over spring break and my daughter, Sophie, really, really, really wanted to go with me. I asked my son, Noah, if he wouldn't mind staying home with his dad. Actually, he preferred staying home. Noah is challenged with autism. Although he is very high on the spectrum, traveling, crowds, crying babies, among other things, make it difficult for him. Knowing that this would not be a vacation, he chose to stay back. As his mom, I always wanted to include him and give him the option.

If Noah wanted to join us, I would have purchased him a ticket as well.

I jumped online to found some decently priced tickets on Alaska Airlines. Sophie and I would fly from Ketchikan to San Francisco on March 31. If I remember correctly, I booked one-way tickets because I was not sure of my brother's condition. It would be easier to book return flights once we had a better idea of what we were dealing with.

The second trip took place on August 2 through August. It was because of Ron's reaction to this trip that my sister and I started planning some way for the kids and me to leave Ketchikan safely. Ronald's behavior was totally unhinged. He was beyond irrational. I was traveling to San Francisco on my own this time, and the children were left with him.

On August 2, I flew from Ketchikan, Alaska to San Francisco, California.

"Who's going to pick you up?" Ron irritably asked.

"Andrea will ask Bri to," I answered, curious as to why he even cared.

Bri is Charlie's sister-in-law. She drove up from San Diego the week prior to help. Upon arriving in San Francisco, I received a text from Andrea. She asked if I didn't mind taking a taxi because Bri had to get on the road. She had an eight-hour drive ahead of her and had to be back to work the next morning.

From the time that I arrived at the terminal and was going to baggage claim, Ron was constantly texting and checking on me. I told him to calm down and that once I got my bag and got to Charlie's house, then I would call him. I didn't even think to mention that I would take a taxi; God forbid!

After collecting my suitcase, I arranged a car from the taxi service. I called Ron from the car— big mistake! As soon as he found out I was taking a taxi, he LOST it! I mean, he truly, unequivocally LOST his senses. He started screaming at the top of his voice, lecturing me, and demanding to know the driver's name, license plate, make and model of the vehicle, etc. He was so loud and so irrationally intense that he even made the driver nervous, so I just hung up.

He was fuming! Ron was so enraged that I would ever do that to him, he started ranting to the children that I was a liar, and—well, let's just say he used some very vile vocabulary. He said that everything I did was a lie. My daughter, Sophia, God Bless her, secretly recorded his outbursts to show me what was going on at home. In the recording, the kid's dad was accusing me of lying about my brother's cancer, just so I could take a trip to California! Please remember, although the kids were teenagers, Noah and Sophie were still young. Sophie was fourteen and Noah sixteen.

I was in shambles that night. My brother was fighting for his life, and my husband was acting insane! I reached out to Ronald's family, asking them all for help. He has four siblings and two grown children. I explained that I needed someone to fly to Ketchikan to be with Noah and Sophie and that I would purchase their ticket. Not one, I repeat, NOT ONE stepped up to the plate to help. They all responded with, "I'm sorry Jess, this is just Ronnie. Give him some time to cool off," or similar words. The responses were via text. No one even bothered to pick up the phone to check on us.

I immediately forwarded my texts and the recordings to Ronald's psychiatrist. I also called my friend Jean to see if she could somehow help with the kids while I was gone. Dr. Russ Ward and I discussed a safety plan for the kids during the time I would be away. It suffices to say, both Sophie and Noah would end up staying with Jean and Emma the entire week I was gone.

"Okay, so he can't admit how off-base he is. Then it's definitely time to go if he can't or won't acknowledge his issues. No amount of therapy will help. He will be this way until the day he dies." My sister Grace was responding to a text I sent her.

The plan was for Tyler to come up for a visit. Like I mentioned before, this would not be unusual. Since it was August, the late summer salmon run would be starting. I would book ferry tickets for myself, the kids, the dog, Ty, and my SUV. Over the course of the week, we would quietly pack a few belongings, tucking them aside. This would include important documents (passports, birth certificates, school records, etc.). I had a seasonal part-time position, so the morning that we were to board the ferry, I would make an excuse for Tyler to take me to work, suggesting that the kids and dog join us so we could grab a bite for breakfast. Our golden absolutely loves car rides, so having Stella jump in for a ride would not be anything out of the ordinary.

In my ideal world, the plan would work. Actually, in my ideal world, my marriage would be amazing, and I would not even be writing these words. Unfortunately, this was not the case.

Ronald liked to sleep in, and by the time he noticed that no one was coming back to the house at a reasonable time, the ferry would have already left. Jean's concern was that many things could go wrong as the week progressed. Her initial, and most probable, fear was that once Ron realized we were gone, he would figure out that we were on the ferry, jump on a plane, and be at the ferry dock at its next stop along the southern route. As their father, Ronald might have the right to deny my taking the kids out of state, or at least use that against me. Noah and Sophie were minors at the time. Although Ron and I were not separated or divorced, he would use the threat of that to manipulate and control me. He knew that if I wanted a divorce, he could force me to stay in Ketchikan with no other family as support, simply because he would insist on staying—and I would NEVER leave my children!

Jean did make a valid point.

"You're right," I responded, "but what else can I do?"

"We'll figure this out, don't worry, hun," Jean said, giving me a reassuring hug.

Going to pick Tyler up, the girls and I hopped back in the car, heading to the airport first with the promised stop at the coffee shop. As fate had it, Ty's flight was delayed by close to two hours. By the time he landed and got his bag, it was after 9:30 p.m. I had been texting Ron the flight updates and asked that he make sure Noah had some dinner, since we would be getting back later than expected. He told me that he would. Also, he informed me that he was tired and would probably be asleep when we got in.

On the way back, we, once again, stopped by Miss Jean's house to drop off Emma. I introduced my nephew to Jean. Taking the opportunity during our brief conversation, she also aired her concerns to Tyler about "the plan." I believe he was on the same page.

When we arrived back at the house, Ronald was fast asleep. We had noticed that he had consumed two large bottles of wine, in addition to taking the daily medications for his PTSD. We were quiet but did not tiptoe around. I did not want to disturb him, but Ron's sleeping pattern was one that if he heard us, he would sleep more soundly. The quieter the house became, the more unrestful he was.

The normalcy of anyone just arriving for a visit took place. I showed Ty to his room. Noah came out to say "hi" to his cousin, Sophie sat on Ty's bed to catch up, and I put some munchies out so we could wind down.

"Jess, can I talk to you?" Tyler said.

"Sure, is everything okay? Do you need extra towels or…?"

"No, it's not that. Hey, Sophe, I need to talk with your mom for a bit. Why don't you go upstairs? We'll both be up shortly."

Sophie headed upstairs with her pajamas in hand. Ty would use her bedroom, and my daughter would camp on the living room couch for the week.

"What's up?" I asked.

"Something doesn't feel right, like your house seems off. Don't get me wrong, you have a beautiful home. I'm just sensing that something bad might happen." At this point, Tyler seemed nervous and was sweating profusely.

My nephew had had a long day. After all, he just flew from Chicago to Ketchikan, Alaska, with two changes in-between.

Concerned, I asked, "Are you sure you're not just over tired? It has been quite the travel day."

"No, Jess, I have had this kinda feeling before and," Ty paused, "I know I need to listen to my gut! Hey, I don't want to scare you or anything. It's totally your call, but I think we need to leave tonight. Ron is passed out, and this is—in a weird way—a gift. Your friend, Emma's mom—"

"Jean," I finished his sentence.

"I do agree with her," Tyler continued. "Anything can happen between now and when we are booked on the ferry!"

WOW, I was increasingly getting scared, and something told me to listen. I didn't say anything at first. I just listened, trying to process what was going on. I tried to dismiss the idea all together, thinking, *well, let's just sit down and get some food in us and, maybe, hopefully, we can let this slide and tomorrow when we wake up things will be "normal."*

Sophia came back downstairs and jumped on the bed. She and Tyler turned on the television. This was a nice distraction. I went upstairs to check on Noah. In my mind, I was convincing myself to let Ty's concerns go and just let things be; however, halfway up the flight of stairs, something stopped me. It wasn't a voice. It was such a strong feeling in the pit of my stomach, telling me, "No," SCREAMING for me to turn around and listen to my nephew.

Turning around, I went back into the kids' room. Sophia and Tyler had been chatting. They both looked at me when I walked back in. I told Sophie to turn the volume up a little bit on the television. Background noise would comfort Ron, making him think we were still at the house.

"Jess, what do you want to do? What's the plan?" whispered my nephew.

"I think you are right. We need to leave while he is passed out. Ty, help Sophie pack a small duffle and put your things in the back of the SUV. I'm not going to say anything to your brother. I will gather a few things myself and get him right before we are ready to leave. Until then, just act as normal as possible, just in case he does wake up." My heart was pounding. I knew once we walked out that door, my life would never be the same again.

I quietly went back upstairs to put my bathrobe on over my clothes. As I gathered a few belongings, I made sure to make it look as though I was making up the living room couch for Sophia and washing up for bed. At one point, Ron rolled over to reach for me in the bed. I quickly sat on the edge of the bed and rubbed his arm, letting him know I was there.

Consoling my husband, I said in a whisper, "Hey sweetie, I'll be to bed soon; just getting everyone settled."

Ronald rolled back on his side, snoring again.

I brought my things downstairs and had Tyler put them in the car. The layout of the house allowed for us to access the garage from the foyer, with Sophia's bedroom being right off the foyer on the lower level, as well.

"Okay guys, get in the car. I'll go up and have Noah come down. Sophie, sweetie, did you pack a few things for your brother?" Again, my heart was pounding in disbelief of what I was about to do.

"Yes," my sweet daughter said. "Wait!"

"What?" Ty shrugged his shoulders.

"I need to get one more thing." My daughter ran back into her room. She had the biggest crush on Justin Bieber, and she wanted to take her 2018 Justin Bieber calendar with her.

"Seriously, Sophe!" exclaimed her cousin.

Sophia giggled nervously.

At this point, Tyler, Sophia, and Stella, our golden retriever, were in the car waiting. I went upstairs and knocked on Noah's door. He was in his pajamas, reading. I asked him to go downstairs to say good night to his cousin. Initially, Noah was reluctant.

"Oh, come on, sweetie," I said. "Your cousin just traveled all the way from the Midwest to spend some time with you. Why don't you bring down your gaming system to show him?"

"Hmmm… Okay," he mumbled.

"Hey sweetie, where is your laptop?"

"Why?" Noah asked, giving me a funny look.

"Ty might want to see that as well."

"Whatever." Noah picked up his electronics and headed downstairs. I followed closely behind.

It was obvious that my son had no clue what was going on. As we descended the stairwell, I explained to him that we needed to leave and that this was the safest way. To my surprise, Noah was fairly calm.

I manually opened the garage door so as not to make too much noise. We put the vehicle in neutral and pushed it out, not starting the engine until we were at the edge of the driveway.

"Where to now?" asked my nephew anxiously.

"The Safe House."

Ketchikan has a women's safe house. Earlier in the summer, when life in my own home was becoming more and more toxic, I had reached out for help. I had never been to the facility but had quietly made arrangements to speak with their counselors regarding my situation. Between my earlier conversations with Ronald's psychiatrist and the few meetings I had previously with Miss Shelly from the shelter, the center seemed to be expecting us when we arrived.

"Where is it?" Ty asked

"I actually don't know. Sophe, can you call Miss Jean for me? She will know."

It was now about 1:30 a.m. The night seemed endless. I was exhausted and a nervous wreck. Noah was beginning to have a panic attack, wanting to turn back around and go home. I did not blame him. Part of me wanted to just give up and go back to my beautiful house, even if it meant walking on eggshells for the rest of my life. This was the hardest decision I had to make, because it did not just involve me; I was changing the course for my children as well.

I knew with every ounce of my being we couldn't go back. I knew that Ronald would play the victim in all of this, twisting everything. He was a master of manipulation.

When we arrived at the safe house, one of the counselors on duty took the children to a family room to get them settled in for the night. My nephew stayed with me in the office while I explained our situation and started filling out paperwork. We waited for a police officer to arrive to take our statements and figure out what options we had.

Over the next hour or so, Ronald woke up and realized we were gone. In a major panic, he started calling and texting. He was concerned, confused, angry, and outraged. *How dare they leave me!* I could only imagine the dialogue going through his brain.

I honestly don't remember how we responded to my husband. Everything happened so fast. I dug ever so deep, using every ounce of strength so as not to have a nervous breakdown. I needed to be strong for my kids. I needed to make it out of this madness. I felt as though I was being consumed by the flames of hell.

How does anyone go through something like this, let alone survive this? My mind raced.

What I do remember is that the officer and the counselors immediately showed us how to turn off the location settings/GPS on our phones. They also moved my SUV, so Ron would not be able to spot it from the street.

Apparently, while I was trying to sort things out in my

brain, Ronald was in our little red mustang searching for us. The police dispatch had eyes on him all over town, even though they had informed Ronald that we were safe.

"Mr. Millard, your wife, and children have been in contact with us. They are safe. We have an officer speaking with them now. It is best that you return home until we can determine the situation." The police had called Ronald. I had given them both his cell number as well as the land line number.

"Ms. Millard, do you have any family in town where you and the children can stay? Anyone at all?" Officer Crawly asked.

"No," I replied, holding back tears.

"Your husband is not being reasonable, and it is not safe for you to stay here in Ketchikan." The officer and the counselors discussed the options.

"Do you have any family anywhere else in Alaska? Maybe Juneau or Anchorage?" they continued.

These were legitimate questions, but we had no family in Alaska. All of our family were back in the lower 48.

"Ms. Millard, why don't you and the children try to get some sleep? We will plan to fly you out in the morning.

You mentioned you have a brother in San Francisco?" The counselor, Ms. Shelly, was trying to console me.

"But I don't have any money. What am I doing?" I asked, fearing the worst.

I had $5.00 in my wallet and a credit card, of which both Ronald and I were on the account. I knew, I just knew deep down, that Ron would not rise to the occasion and be concerned for our welfare. He did what I feared he would do. He canceled the only credit card I had on me and emptied out our joint bank account. For a man who truly cared about his wife and children—he left us penniless! Maybe he figured if I did not have access to the finances, I would come crawling home, asking for forgiveness?

It was 8:30 a.m. I must have fallen asleep on one of the couches. I looked over and saw both Noah and Sophia fast asleep on another couch, covered by a soft, but tattered, duvet. The Safe House is just that. It is a place for women and families to come to be safe. Nothing fancy, but it is secure.

I smelled coffee and walked downstairs to the office. The morning staff had arrived and been filled in on our case. What an absolutely wonderful group of women. They greeted me with a smile, offering me a much-needed cup of coffee! I didn't even notice that my nephew had stepped out. Earlier in the morning, one of the staff had told Tyler that the only way we could fly with our dog was to get her a crate for the airlines. He took it upon himself to call our local vet and arranged to "borrow" a crate for our flight.

"Ms. Millard?" inquired the counselor.

"Yes" I responded

"I have booked you on the 11:30 a.m. flight from Ketchikan to Seattle. You will have a seven-hour layover in Seattle with a connecting flight to San Francisco," she informed me. "Because of the length of the layover, you will need to pick up Stella and then check her back in an hour before your connecting flight."

"Oh my God! Thank you so much. Thank you for everything that you have done for us!" I was so appreciative, yet numb, like a shell of a person.

I felt like an empty vessel, frail and vulnerable. BUT this was not the time to think. Now was the time for me to trust those who cared about our well-being and not step back into denial.

At 10:00 a.m., a taxi arrived to take us to the airport. I left my SUV and the keys with the police so that Ronald could arrange to pick it up. Because of the security issues and the possibility of family violence, Alaska State Troopers were stationed at the two entrances to our very small airport terminal. The agent at the desk had been expecting us. She promptly checked us in and escorted us past TSA. The kids were relieved, I was numb, and my nephew—well, he got more excitement than anyone should ever need to handle.

Boarding that plane was by no means the end. It was just the beginning. We were about to step into another layer of madness—what felt like hell!

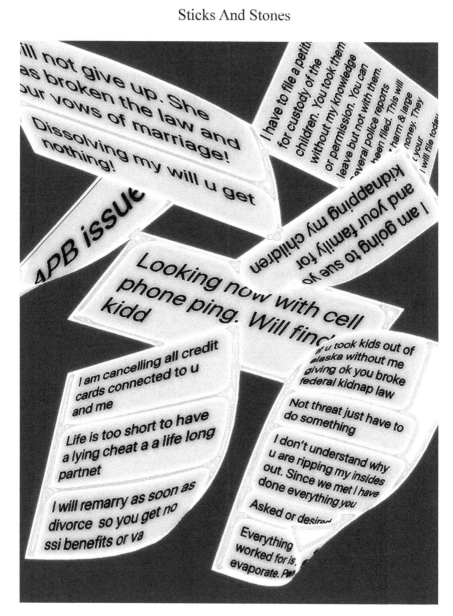

Run, but You Can't Hide

The following are texts that flooded in from Ron in the early morning of August 20:

If u took kids out of Alaska without me giving ok you broke federal kidnap law.
Not threat just have to do something.

I don't understand why u are ripping my insides out. Since we met I have done everything for you.

Asked or desired.

Everything we have worked for is going to evaporate. Penniless.

You cannot take Noah and Sophia. I will find them.

Hiring a PI in San Fran and here that I will help. You are breaking the law.

Looking now with cell phone ping. Will find kids.

APB issued!

I am going to sue you and your family for kidnapping my children.

I am coming to find you Noah and Sophie. Try and let me know if you are alive and where. Your mother has gone crazy and may hurt u!

I will not give up. She has broken the law and our vows of marriage!

Dissolving my will u get nothing!

I have to file a petition for custody of the children. You took them without my knowledge or permission. You can leave but not with them. Several police reports have been filed. This will cost great harm and large amounts of money. They are not just your children. I will file today.

Best to tell Tyler to disappear or whoever you are running with!

I am canceling all credit cards connected to u and me.

Life is too short to have a lying cheat as a life long partner.

I will remarry as soon as divorce so you get nothing!

From the Frying Pan into the Fire

August 20

"Ladies and Gentlemen, we are starting our descent into the Seattle area. The weather is sunny and a beautiful eighty-two degrees with a slight wind coming in from the southeast." I heard the co-pilot making an announcement over the intercom.

I had fallen asleep. The flight from Ketchikan to Seattle was two and a half hours long. Once we boarded the plane and took our seats, it did not surprise me one bit that we all passed out from sheer exhaustion. The events leading up to last night's departure were traumatic, to say the least. I was relieved, yet I knew that there were going to be very difficult consequences to face. Ronald was not rational. He would not make life easy. But I would cross that bridge when it came. Right now, I just wanted to get my children and myself to San Francisco and closer to my family.

"Ladies and Gentlemen," the stewardess made the arrival announcement, "we will be landing in Seattle shortly.

Please put your tray tables away and return your seat backs to their upright position. Thank you for joining us on Alaska Airlines today and enjoy your stay in the Seattle area."

During the flight, prior to closing my eyes and passing out, Tyler and I discussed travel options. Although the Ketchikan Safe House had booked us flights to San Francisco, we had a seven-hour layover in Seattle, we had a dog in a carrier, and two children whose nerves were frayed. My son, Noah, challenged with autism, was fragile when it came to airports, crowds, travel, and the like. We were also concerned that Ronald might be on the next flight out of Ketchikan to track us down. My nephew and I came up with a new plan to throw him off the scent, so to speak.

"Kids," Ty said with a humorous tone, "how 'bout a road trip?"

"What do you mean?" Sophie asked, a bit confused. "Aren't we going to Uncle Charlie's house?"

"Yup! But instead of waiting around at the airport for seven hours, we're going to drive twelve!" Ty rolled his eyes.

"Sure!" Noah exclaimed in relief. "I like that idea better. Then I don't have to deal with people."

From the Frying Pan into the Fire

We had to pick up Stella anyhow from the agents at baggage claim. We would let them know that we had a family emergency (which indeed we did) and that we needed to get our luggage off in Seattle, even though it had been checked through to San Francisco.

"I hope that won't be a problem?" I was muttering to myself as I was trying to work through any hiccups our new plan might prompt.

When the wheels of the plane touched down, we all seemed to, at the very same moment, turn off the "airplane mode" on our cell phones.

Texts come flooding in:

Called Cops!

No Reason to disappear

I will report the suv as stolen. Your name
is not on the mustang loan / title or the
home original extended VA home loan.
You will lose all VA & Social Security benefits from me I will fight you for
custody of kids. You will start over at 55+

with no career. This I promise is coming down your road. Gave it all to you and you "&%$@#" in my mouth. They will have to go all through it with you …

Everything we worked for is going to evaporate. Penniless.

You cannot take Noah and Sophie. I will find them.

You cannot hide my children from me. What is wrong with you?

You will be arrested

Missing persons-report being filed right now

Filed - any accessory to this crime will be charged as well!

All coming to an end. You win destruction of our marriage. Congrats

From the Frying Pan into the Fire Princess

This is the worst thing you could have done to me. You killed me Jessica and your childrens father!

Everything is for sale for you to move. I just don't understand. I am a good father and husband.

Jess you and Noah and Sophe are my only friends. I love you all! Please don't leave me. I will be perfect (praying hands emoji)

I will leave the front door unlocked in case you don't hear back from me. Do not let our beautiful home be ruined

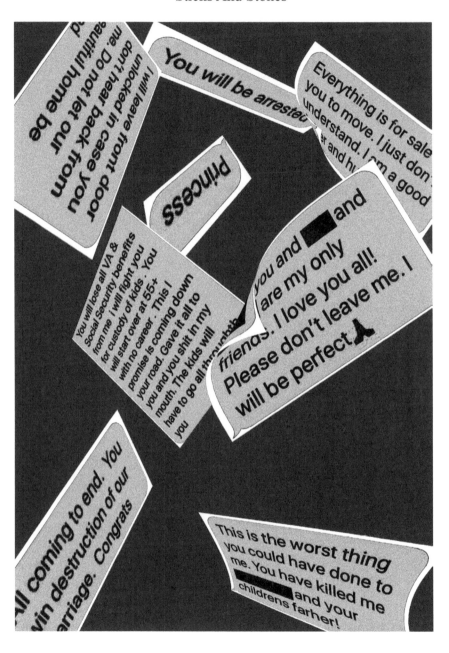

His threats hit me like a sledgehammer. My nephew noticed that I sat back down as tears were swelling up in my eyes. He took my phone from me and glanced over the messages.

"Jess," Tyler said, encouraging me to get up. "You must ignore Ron. This is a total crock! He is just trying to manipulate you—empty threats. You have done nothing wrong. In fact, you have done everything right, and the law is behind you. He knows it; that is why he is so desperate."

I pulled myself together, and the four of us got off the plane. Once in the terminal, we headed to baggage claim to pick up our sweet Stella and speak with the agents to hopefully (fingers crossed) have them pull off our luggage in Seattle. This did not go quite as smoothly as planned; however, we did get Stella, and three out of four of the duffle bags. Of course, the bag they could not track down was mine. I thought, *oh well, hopefully we will reunite in San Francisco.*

As it was getting late in the day, Ty and I decided to find a pet-friendly hotel for the evening. We would take a cab from the airport and book a rental car once we were at the hotel. The kids and the dog were relieved to stop for the day.

Thank goodness! After thirty minutes of non-stop calls, I finally found a hotel for the evening. They were reasonably priced, CLEAN, and dog- friendly. My nephew booked two rooms. I don't know what I would have done without my family's help emotionally as well as financially. By family, I mean my sister, Grace, and my nephew, Tyler. They insisted that I not worry about anything. The most important thing was that the kids and I were safe.

"It will take some time, but we will get through this as a family," my sister kept telling me. "I love you, and God forbid if he ever hurt you or the kids, I would never forgive myself!"

Earlier in the summer, Grace had a nightmare. She woke up in a sweat! When her husband, Gene, asked what was wrong, she told him that she dreamt that the kids and I had gone missing. In the dream, there was a headline in the news, "Missing Mother and Children Found DEAD!"

"He did it!" she exclaimed. "Ron is going to drag them somewhere remote and get rid of them."

Grace was almost in a panic as Gene wrapped his arms around her to comfort her.

"They will be fine," he insisted. "It was just a dream."

"No—I don't have a good feeling about this." She

wept. "You didn't see how Jessie looked. When I saw her this last trip, I didn't know who looked worse: my brother, who is fighting cancer, or my sister!"

Once checked in at the hotel, with showers and pizza ordered; everyone could rest except for me. I needed to arrange a one-way rental car from Seattle to San Francisco. Tyler booked the car using his credit card. I didn't have any money on me, but even if I did have my credit card, Ronald would be able to track its use.

Everyone said goodnight, and Ty went to his room. I just sat in a big plush chair in the corner of the hotel room. With my knees tucked into my chest, I cuddled up and watched the kids and dog fast asleep in bed. My mind was vacant. I honestly didn't know what I was thinking or feeling. How do I even begin to wrap my head around this?

I know I'm not crazy, I kept telling myself. *This was the only way. How many more years? How much more damage to the kids?"*

"You know that when you leave, you will just have to go. You know you can't ever come back. You will have to leave it ALL behind. Do you think you can do this?" asked my friend Lee. "It is the only way—to keep you and the kids safe."

Ketchikan was a tight-knit community. It was small and everybody seemed to know everybody else's business. I thought I was good at portraying a home-life that was typical and healthy, but apparently not. As optimistic and involved in the community as I was, my friends knew something was off. They knew I would overachieve to accommodate for what was lacking.

Captain Ron was only known—hmmm, how do I describe this? My husband was a very hard worker. He strived to provide for his family. He was known in the circles where he worked, but rarely would participate in the kid's school events, after-school activities, or any other kind of social engagements. He would tell me that was my job. This seemed amiss to me; however, after years of marinating in someone else's mindset, I became accustomed to savoring whatever breadcrumbs he would throw my way.

Looking around the hotel room, I desperately tried to comprehend what was going on.

"God, thank you!" I whispered, tears now streaming down my cheeks. "Please, please, please, get us through this unscathed!"

The next morning came, and I had to pinch myself. This was REAL! The kids were still asleep, so I jumped in to take a LONG, HOT shower. We had a long drive ahead of us. We booked a midsize SUV through Enterprise. Yes, I'm going to shamelessly plug their name because, as their ad says: "Enterprise picks you up." They did. With a long drive ahead, four tall people and a dog, we opted to upgrade to a full-size SUV. The gal assisting us was awesome. I'm not sure what story or version of our story Tyler told her, but the upgrade was at no extra charge. "Thank you, Jesus!"

I started the drive, however, after living on an island for fifteen years with only thirty miles of road, I was getting a bit nervous driving through heavy traffic—city traffic. Before Ron moved us to Alaska, before I even knew my husband existed, I was a seasoned traveler. I was in the fashion industry and had been privileged to live abroad for over a decade, traveling around the globe on locations. I would jump in my car and drive from Boston to New York City without hesitation. I was a bit rusty, so Tyler insisted on taking over.

"Jess, let me drive. There will be plenty of open road later on where you can take over."

"Yes, of course—thank you." I pulled over into a convenience store parking lot.

God paved the way.

Tyler was an atheist growing up. I was uncertain of his faith now that he was a young adult; however, he knew that my relationship with Jesus was important to me. He also encouraged me to hold on to my faith if that was what was needed to give me the strength to get through this.

Three wondrous signs confirmed that we were on the correct path. Three signs from God that I believe today not only cemented my faith but planted a seed in Ty's heart.

Leaving the Seattle area as we were getting on the I-5, Sophia pointed out a billboard sign.

"Mom, look!" she exclaimed.

"What is it, sweetie?"

"The billboard; look what it says." Sophe was my churchgoing, Jesus-praising buddy.

Turning my head to look at where she was pointing was a HUGE sign that said: "TRUST IN JESUS."

"Oh, Lord, I do," I said out loud. "I do."

Tyler smiled and responded in a very sweet manner, "See, auntie, it'll be okay. Your Jesus will take care of you."

I turned and looked back at the kids. Noah had his headphones on and was listening to music. Sophie's beautiful young face was pressed against the window as she just stared out. I could only imagine what she was thinking.

"Well, kiddos. We've got a long drive ahead. Sit back, get comfortable, and enjoy the ride." Their cousin was doing a fabulous job cheering them up and turning this tragedy into an adventure.

Twelve hours is only half a day, but twelve hours sitting in a car can do some damage to one's behind. Seriously, though, the road trip was going well. We stayed on I-5 to make decent time, and some of the scenery was quite pretty—especially when we were going through parts of Oregon. It was when we were about to cross the California border that my daughter brought up an interesting subject. Possibly something we should be concerned about.

"Where is Redding, California?" Sophie asked.

"Northern California, I think—we can look it up. Why?" I asked.

"You know those fires that have been happening in California? It says that they are jumping the roads and part of I-5 has been closed." She was reading some posts on Snap Chat.

"Oh—! That's right," Ty said. "Is San Fran North or South of Redding?"

"I think we have to go through it," she said apprehensively.

"Are you sure?" I jumped in.

"Well, we'll just keep driving south and pray that we don't have to." Tyler came back with a new mindset. He was determined to deliver us to San Francisco and get on the next flight back to Chicago. Not that he had had enough of us, just that he had a girlfriend waiting for him at home.

The bright blue skies and sweet fragrant air slowly started changing. As we continued southbound, there was a haze that started consuming the surroundings. It was not city pollution, but rather the smoke from fires. The wind had carried it North, and although the fires were in California, Oregon was feeling its wrath. So far, there had been no warnings or indications of road closures. We kept our eyes peeled just in case a detour was up ahead. The traffic seemed to thin out. The further south we traveled, the fewer number of cars were traveling with us.

"Feels kinda eerie," Tyler commented

"I agree." I continued, "Do you think we should find another route to take?"

My nephew stayed on I-5. The skies got darker and the smoke thicker. You could feel it in your lungs. Now, we didn't see any cars. It appeared we had made a huge mistake and probably should have turned off a while back.

"HADES Bound!" Ty exclaimed. "Nothing like jumping from the pan into the fire—literally."

The sarcasm was almost a relief. It was at that very moment a black pickup truck came speeding up from behind. Tyler had noticed its lights in the rearview mirror. They seemed to be flickering on and off, but it was an illusion because of the smoke-filled air. As it got closer, it pulled over to the left lane and passed us at a rather hefty speed. We were still traveling at seventy mph, so this vehicle couldn't have been going less than eighty-five mph. What grabbed our attention was that as soon as it passed, it pulled over in front of us in our lane and slowed down.

Holy—! Look at what is in the back of the truck," my nephew said in disbelief. "Your God MUST be real."

As the truck moved over in front of us, blocking out its entire rear cab window, was a sign that said: "FOLLOW JESUS."

My body was covered in chills. I knew this was God leading us through the flames. As fast as the truck had appeared, it vanished into the smoke ahead.

We never did find a detour, but eventually the air cleared and our route on I-5 remained open.

"Are you tired, Tyler? I can do some driving for a bit."

"Sure," he sighed. "Let's stop and fuel up and get some food. We'll change then."

We had been alternating the driving, however, this last stretch seemed to wear him out.

"Do you want to stop for the night instead?" I was concerned the day was getting too long for us all and that pushing it wasn't the best idea.

"I'd rather get you there tonight so I can fly home tomorrow. Otherwise, it's just another day of this nightmare for me—no offense," he wearily remarked.

"None taken."

By the time we reached the outskirts of San Francisco, it was past 11:00 p.m. We had been looking to book a hotel for the night. My brother was back in the hospital, and I didn't want to bring all our troubles onto my sister-in-law's doorstep.

"There is a hotel in Northern San Fran. Why don't we book a couple rooms there? Its dog- friendly," I suggested.

From the Frying Pan into the Fire

We made the call and got two rooms. I texted Andrea to let her know our whereabouts.

"Good luck," she typed back.

"What do you mean?" I asked.

"Northern San Fran isn't the best area …?" I could sense her hesitation.

I read Andrea's response to Tyler. We looked at each other and both agreed—too tired now, so we'll take our chances.

Okay, remember when I was so thrilled with the hotel we stayed at in Seattle? Well, to put it mildly, this hotel needed a major overhaul. It was SCARY. I felt as though we were staying in a red-light district! The door to our room didn't even lock all the way. We had to wedge a chair under the door handle to make sure someone wouldn't just walk in. My nephew went to check and see if his room was any better. Not even two minutes later, he was back.

"You guys got the luxury suite," he retorted "Good luck was right."

We slept in our clothes on top of the covers and tried not to touch anything. The kids were so tired, and I was beyond tired, but there was no way I was going to sleep.

It was now 3:30 a.m. I went online and found a beautiful hotel near where Andrea and my brother live. It was 5-star and was pet friendly. It was a bit expensive, so I texted my sister to see if it would be okay to book.

"Absolutely! In fact, see if you can stay there for the next four days. We want you and the kids to be comfortable and safe until we can figure out the next step." Grace was determined to make sure the kids and I felt as though we weren't a burden. The last thing she wanted was for me to cave and return to Alaska.

We booked a wonderful room at a much nicer hotel. At this point, we needed some sanity in our lives and this hotel provided just that.

With new accommodations booked for the next few days, I still couldn't sleep. Ronald had access to all my accounts (e-mail, Facebook, WIX website, you name it) and he was spreading lies across the internet. I conjured up the mental fortitude to go through each account methodically and change my passwords. This definitely took my mind off of the nasty room we were in.

Having access to my accounts, Ronald wrote this on my Facebook page (as if I would really post something like this?):

From the Frying Pan into the Fire

Jess and Tyler have kidnapped Noah and Sophie without my permission. I have filed a police report and am bring it to the FBI as well. Illegal and all involved could be charged.

The next morning, as soon as the sun was up, Ty was at our door.

"Come on," he said. "Let's get the h— out of here. We'll grab some breakfast and I'll take you to Charlie's."

"Change of plans." I filled him in on the new hotel. "Let's go straight there and see if they can check us in early."

While heading over to the new hotel, Tyler got a text from my sister. She was able to book him on an afternoon flight from San Francisco to Chicago. Grace knew her son was champing at the bit to get home and since we were in a safe, clean hotel for a few days —needless to say, my sister and I were both very proud of how Tyler jumped in to help.

We arrived at the hotel. They had a valet and all the amenities of a 5-star hotel. Walking around the car and approaching the glass entrance doors, all four of us saw a gentleman standing near the entrance. He was holding a sign which brought tears to my eyes. The sign said, "Jesus LOVES you." I swear at that moment, he looked our way and winked. God is with us!

A Long and Winding Road

"You gotta be %@*$ kidding me!" my sister, Grace, was screaming on the phone. "What are you thinking? You seriously can't expect Jess and the kids AND a dog to move in with our eighty-year-old aunt?"

Our Auntie Mari is a retired physician. She has a lovely home in Georgia and has always lived by herself. Our oldest sister, Natalie, had suggested we move in with Auntie Mari. For an onlooker, this might sound like a reasonable idea, but we knew our other sister's motives. She was protecting her own interests. Natalie didn't want us to be anywhere near her in California as she thought she might get stuck having to help us out.

"I was just thinking that…" Nat calmly tried to explain her position.

"Never mind." Grace took a deep breath to calm her nerves. "I get it. Jess needs our help, and her situation is inconvenient for you right now."

Don't get me wrong, our eldest sister is wonderful, but sometimes her way of thinking can be—a bit self-centered?

"Gene and I will figure this out, but remember, you DON'T own California!" Grace slammed down the phone.

August 21

The kids and I settled into our beautiful hotel room. In the midst of this nightmare, God provided a reprieve—a place to stop for a few days until long-terms plans could be made.

I was so tired, so frail, and weary; I just wanted to collapse, but I knew I couldn't. What I could do was rest for at least a little while. We all took turns taking long, hot showers. The kids put on their jammies; I changed into the robe provided by the hotel. Remember, my bag was the one that we could not retrieve in Seattle, so I have been wearing the same outfit for a couple of days now.

"Mom," Noah caught my attention. "Can we get some food—I'm starving!"

"Absolutely—look, they have room service." I responded. "Let's get something brought up. I don't want to go anywhere right now."

The kids ordered food, put on the television, and passed out. Stella found her spot and was upside down and snoring. *Oh, the life of a dog,* I think to myself. I found myself sitting in yet another cozy loveseat at the corner of the hotel room, making a list of things to do and people to call.

"Are you and the kids okay?" My sister Grace was the first person on the phone. "Sweetie, if you and the kids are comfortable there, Gene and I would like you to stay a few extra days until we can sort something out." She paused and then added, "We are seriously thinking of having you guys move out to Michigan with us. We live in a small community. You can use this as a base, get the kids registered into school and you have family near to help you get back on your feet. Charlie is in the hospital, and, well, Nat made her opinion known, so probably best not to stay in San Francisco."

At this point, I was open to any and all suggestions. I was just so grateful that we were finally away from Ron.

"Sure, that is probably best," I responded as my stomach knotted up. "I can't thank you enough for everything you are doing for us. I feel like such a failure. I don't know why I let it go on for so long—get so bad."

"You did nothing WRONG, remember that." Grace tried to counsel me. "You are a sweet, smart, kind woman and he knew how to use that against you. If you didn't have the strength to get out for yourself, well, you did it for your kids. They will thank you someday."

Journal Entry:

Living under the thumb of a narcissist—

It is amazing … almost frightening … how powerful a word can be. Delivered with emotion … words become tangible. They can be used to comfort or … on the opposite side … manipulate and destroy.

Words, when fueled by anger, can be dangerous … are dangerous.

One can only imagine how damaging a twenty year marriage was when words were used to control and manipulate. These very

words backed by body language became
the prison that held this family captive for
so many years.

Sticks and stones might break my bones
but WORDS (will never hurt me). Think
again—Words can KILL!

The scars go deeper than the flesh. The
scars altered the way I thought and felt. It
got to the point that I was always questioning myself.

Forget about learning to walk on eggshells.
I mastered walking on hand grenades!

Later in the day, I called my sister-in-law to let her
know where we were staying and to check on my brother.
Charlie was in the hospital. Over the course of the last few
months, he had been receiving chemotherapy treatments
for testicular cancer. Although the cancer markers were
down, Charlie's lungs had been compromised by the bleo-

mycin treatments.

"You know, my mom is flying in tomorrow. Maybe she could pick up your bag since she's going to be at the airport anyway?" Andrea suggested.

"Oh, that would be a huge help," I responded. "How is Charlie? I want to see him; do you think he's up for a visit?"

"I know he would be thrilled to see you." Andrea continued, "If you think the kids are safe by themselves at the hotel, mom could swing by, drop off your bag, and pick you up. She was planning to go straight to the hospital anyway. Lynn and I might just join you there as well."

For any typical person, traveling takes planning and coordinating; from booking flights to arranging hotel accommodations and rental cars. Our "trip," however, was thrown together. We had to flee a vile scenario, and now, as the pieces started presenting themselves, I had to tidy things up. I also had to be smart about the "what if's" and prepare for anything. Tyler was right; my husband was desperate, and only God knew if he would try to track us down. Were his words empty threats or real? I wasn't going to take that chance.

I phoned down to the reception and asked to speak with

the manager. I explained our situation and also gave him the phone numbers to the Ketchikan Safe House, as well as the Ketchikan Police, just in case he thought I might be a "nut case." To my relief, the manager was understanding and reassuring.

"Ma'am, you don't have to worry about a thing," he responded. "The floors above the mezzanine are locked and only guests with a hotel key can get access. We can make a note on your account, so if anyone arrives asking for you that you are not expecting, we can quietly alert you as well as security."

"Thank you so much! I can give you a list of names—family—they will be the only ones who should know that we are even here." I continued, "Also, one more favor? I have a rental car in the parking garage. Is there any way that I can have the rental agent pick the car up from the valet?"

"I don't see why not." The manager added, "Why don't you call them now and explain that your situation is sensitive? If anything, they can speak with me, and I will do the walk around with them on your behalf."

You can't imagine how grateful I was. To actually be speaking with someone who cared—a total stranger! All those years, all those threats and lies on how I would NEV-ER be able to survive on my own. The sad truth is, I started believing him.

Ever so slowly, over the years, Ronald would paint this picture of how the world beyond Ketchikan was like a war zone. His verbiage was always critical, always negative, dark, and depressing. At first, the kids and I would politely disagree and counter his version of life with something more positive; however, this would only last so long. He would almost always discredit our views and only allow his opinions to count. For any sane person, it seems simple— believe and defend your own truth. BUT when your ideas are constantly under scrutiny, constantly being questioned, constantly being twisted, and criticized—that can do some major damage.

One more task. With my brother in the hospital and my sister-in-law at home alone with her four-year-old daughter, my family asked me to contact the local authorities. Ron might not know where the kids and I were, but he knew where Charlie and Andrea lived.

This just felt so surreal. This was not my life. This was not the "happily ever after" I dreamt of and worked so hard for. Where did it go wrong? Was I so blinded by his charm? What could I have done differently? The questions flooded my brain. My heart was broken. BUT it was already broken—cracked years before, and all the therapy in the world wasn't getting us anywhere.

I composed this letter a few days prior to the fateful night. I was still trying to make things right and give him the benefit of the doubt. If I could only just reason with him—get through to him! I swear, I was fooling myself. I was desperately holding onto something that never was. It was all a façade.

Ron,

I will start by asking for your forgiveness, your love, and understanding. This is NOT a "Dear John" letter, but rather my heart trying to explain why we need this time away to heal.

I love you! There is no question about that. What I don't love is the two people we have become over the years. No one is to blame; it is just how we grew and survived together.

You are an amazing man. You are and will always be my knight in shining armor. You are a wonderful, trusting, hardworking husband who has always provided and never stopped trying to make things better.

Together, we have accomplished things that others only dream of.
We have two amazing children and a beautiful home.

In our quest to build this life, your undeniable strengths and my ease and ability to adjust my personality to accommodate and support those strengths unfortunately became our undoing. Our balance was fractured. I woke up one day, really not knowing who I had become, and you had lost the optimistic woman you fell in love with years ago.

A Long and Winding Road

Our beautiful home was no longer an
oasis, but rather a prison for me and the
children. I understand and love the fact
that you want to keep us safe. You always
have, but ever so slowly, our home became
your fortress, and the world outside, a
place never to venture...a dark, evil, cruel,
and dangerous place.

You once told me that you fell in love
with me because I could manage to smile
during the most difficult of times. I can
honestly say I have, but when those smiles
too often become tears ...

I know that before we met, we lived very
different lives. You found your way onto
a battlefield, while I was embracing very
much the opposite...a life of beauty and in-
trigue. Yours was dark and mine was light.

It was our sense of adventure that was the common denominator, bringing our two worlds together. What could be, and for the most part was, a perfect balance.

You are strong, and I am not strong enough to keep our balance intact. I could blame this on your PTSD, but rather I would like to just admit, I was too weak to hold my ground ...too afraid of losing your love and respect. And I did just that and more. I not only lost your trust; I lost myself.

In trying to reinsert myself into our relationship, you told me two things: "I don't know who you are," and "you are my problem."

I don't want to be "your problem;" I want to be your loving partner.

A Long and Winding Road

I also found myself pulling away from you, mentally and physically. The distance was the only way I could protect myself from falling back into the pattern of adjusting my personality to suit yours and to keep things calm at home.

Our family is fractured, and the children and I need time to heal so we can mend it before it shatters.

I see a bright future for us all. I always have. One filled with pure joy, laughter, bantering of great ideas, memories made and dreams .... big dreams achieved.

Noah and Sophia need to be able to dream. They need to be able to know both sides of life. Yes, be aware and be safe, but also thrive and not just survive.

Ron, please understand how much we love you. We only need time. I pray for your understanding and for our healing.

With God, we can do this.

Love, in the sincerest meaning of the word,

Jessie

If Ron truly cared about me, truly loved the kids and me, why did he respond with THREATS? Wouldn't a loving, caring husband be concerned? Wouldn't he want to know "what went wrong?" Wouldn't he do everything he could to ease the situation?

I read my note repeatedly. Maybe someday I would send this to him. Maybe someday God will ease his heart and open his eyes, but for now, the letter would stay tucked away inside my journal.

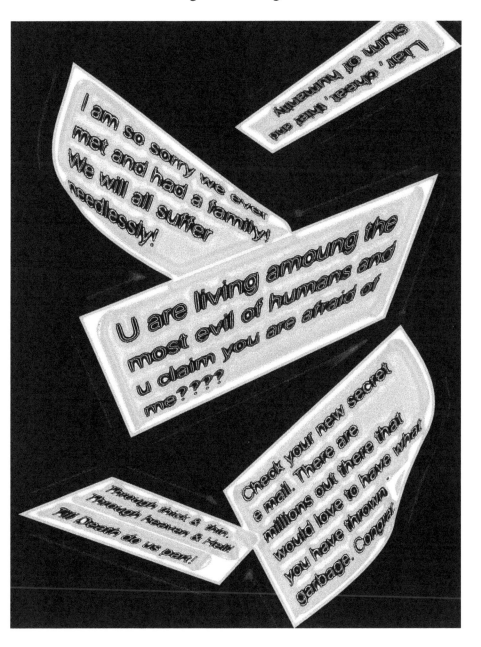

Texts continue flooding in:

I am so sorry we ever met and had a family! We will all suffer needlessly!

Check your new secret e mail. There are
millions out there that would love to
have what you have thrown in garbage.
Congrats!

Liar, cheat, thief, and scum of humanity

Through thick & thin.
Through heaven and Hell!
Till Death do us part!

LEMON MERINGUE PIE

August 20

The kids and our dog were comfortable, hunkered down at the hotel. Shirley, Charlie's mother-in-law, had flown into San Francisco from Palm Desert. Such a doll, she would pick up my lost duffle bag from baggage claim! Thank goodness, now I could have a fresh change of clothes.

The selection of our wardrobe was quite random. The night we left Ketchikan, the only clothing packed was hurriedly thrown together—definitely not a planned trip, but at least they were clean, and they were mine.

"Jess," Shirley suggested, "after we see Charlie, I'll swing you by Target to buy a few things for you and the kids. We're not sure how long you will be staying put. It's a great hotel, so you might as well enjoy the pool and make lemonade out of lemons."

"Thank you sooooo much!" I gave Shirley a huge hug.

"It's going to be okay," she insisted with a confirming smile on her face. "We're family after all, and we look out for one another. Plus, your brother can breathe now that he knows that you and the kids—and, of course, sweet Stella—are here and safe."

Shirley has the most compassionate heart. My brother not only married an amazing woman, Andrea, but he hit the jackpot with his in-laws.

After freshening up and Shirley visiting with the kids, Shirley and I headed over to the hospital. Charlie was admitted earlier in the month and, unfortunately, had not been discharged. The doctors were finding lesions on his lungs from the chemo, and he was having a very difficult time keeping his oxygen saturation levels up.

When I last saw him, he was barely managing at home, and the day I was flying back to Alaska, the family made the call to get him into the ICU.

"Hey, sis," he said with a bright smile. "I wanted you to come back to see me, but I wasn't expecting the dramatics!"

He always knew how to ease the situation.

"Seriously, how are you and the kids doing? You know we are here for you," he continued.

"Thank you," I said, with tears swelling up in my eyes.

"But enough about me—what's this that they won't let you go home? Are you too charming and the nurses will miss you too much?"

"Absolutely!" Andrea came waltzing in carrying a lemon meringue pie. "Your brother keeps everyone on their toes here!"

"Dancing is more like it," Charlie chimed in.

"Pie?" I just gave him that look.

"At least he has a healthy appetite." Andrea smiled as she sat on the hospital bed beside him, opened it up, and handed us each a plastic fork.

"Might as well make lemonade out of lemons," she said.

That saying must run in the family.

We certainly devoured that pie! And our visit lasted for about three hours when the nursing team came in and kicked Shirley and me out.

"Our celebrity needs some rest," the nurse said with

an air of delight. You could just tell how much this nursing staff loved my brother. "Now get your hugs in—and don't forget that autograph. This young man is destined for greatness!"

Shirley and I wrapped up our visit, but not before Miss Lynn came running in. My four-year-old niece came in to see her daddy and wasn't expecting to see Auntie Jessie.

"Wait! What! How did she get here? Where is my Sophie? You can't share my bedroom with me cause Grandma Shirley is."

The sweetness of this child flooded the room. Everyone just beamed.

"Hey sweetness!" Kneeling down, I gave her a tight squeeze. "We came all the way back from Alaska just to see YOU! And guess what?"

"What?" she asked excitedly.

"Your Sophie, scary Noah, and Stella are here too."

"YOU brought your dog?" Lynn asked excitedly. "You know we have a dog!"

Her questions kept rambling on, as a curious four-year-old's would.

Andrea pulled me aside. "Since you and the kids are staying at that swanky hotel nearby, maybe sweetness over there could spend a night or two with you?" she hinted.

"Absolutely!"

"Hey, Jess—now let's go get you and the kids some swimsuits for that pool of yours." Shirley was prompting us to go.

I gave my brother a huge hug.

"Jess?" Charlie called.

"Ya?" I turned to look back at my brother.

"Love you. I'm really glad you are here!"

"Love you, too," I said, once again holding back tears. "It's going to be okay. Seriously, everything is going to be okay!"

"Now it will," he said with a smile.

This would be the last time I saw Charlie conscious. None of us knew how compromised his lungs were.

August 02, 2018

On August 2, my 14-year-old daughter, Sophia, quietly recorded her father's outburst. The children were at home when I called and told Ronald I took a taxi to my brother's house from the airport. Here my brother was fighting for his life, and my husband was acting insanely jealous and controlling.

Audio Transcript:

Sophie: Taxis are safe

Ron (in an aggressive, irritated tone): How do you know?

Sophie: They seem safer than an—

Ron cut her off: I don't know.

Ron: EXACTLY!

Sophie: The airport is not far away from… like Charlie's house.

Lemon Meringue Pie

Ron (talking over his daughter in an argumentative tone): Oh, yes it is!

Sophie (defending herself): No, it's not, no, but I've been to—

Ron (again, cutting Sophia off): The airport is miles and miles from San Francisco.

Sophie: It's like, no, I've actually been to the airport.

Ron (inserting his authority): I've been to the San Francisco airport!

Sophie: It's like twenty minutes away from Charlie's house if, like, you go on the highway.

Ron: NO—no it's not!

Sophie: Yes, it is—it was last time.

Ron: It's way away in farmlands.

Sophie: It is, but there is a highway-like road and it's only twenty minutes away from Charlie's house.

Ronald (changing the subject): I can't believe your mother lied to me. She keeps lying. That's one thing I'm not going to put up with. She keeps lying, lying, lying. She lies every time about what she's doing— [expletive]! Every time she lies, lies, lies!"

THROUGH THE LOOKING GLASS

Have you ever wondered about your purpose in life? I mean, like, why was I born to these parents? Why did I meet this person? Why is it that my sister can play the piano and I am tone deaf?

Everyone has a story. Every living, breathing soul who walks this planet has a story. We do, because we all have a purpose. God created us with freewill, but ultimately, He is in control. He gave us freewill so as to not make us His puppets; rather, for us truly to seek Him out. And our purpose? Somehow, someway, our stories intermingle with others, creating an opportunity for us to know God.

Some of our stories are adventurous, without incident. I say without incident, because these souls have been given a thirst to dare the unknown. Of course, they will come across many challenges, but their challenges are external natural forces—let's just say rock climbing.

Others have inspirational stories. Souls who have come into this world filled with fear and doubt, but through

God's grace, they find the strength to push through and succeed. A very shy, introverted soul is given the gift of an amazing voice and through that gift, he or she blossoms in the spotlight and inspires others to find their purpose.

And then there are the survivors—survivors of self-destructive behavior to survivors of abuse.

I'm not quite sure where my story fits in. It is one of raw emotion, disbelief and, ultimately, running out of options. My story seems to incorporate that of adventure, inspiration, and survival. But, then again, life is all of that and more.

God gave me a really nice life. I was afforded many opportunities that few get to experience in a lifetime. Well, I was, and I wasn't. The opportunities were there; however, they always seemed to be just out of reach. We were afforded a taste, a glimpse, only for it to be snatched away. My sisters and brother and I would always wonder why we were being teased. It was like a carrot dangled in front of us, but we were never fully allowed to embark. It was as if we were on the outside looking in with noses pressed against the glass, watching in awe, but never being invited into this magnificent party.

My father was a genius. He and his sisters were first

generation Americans, as my grandparents immigrated from Greece to America when the Turks invaded. My mother was stunningly beautiful and brilliantly witty herself. She was from North Carolina and the daughter of a tenant farmer. Our upbringing was modest and a true American tale. Dad had a degree in Engineering from the University of New Hampshire. He worked for several companies and eventually started his own in the basement of our home. I remember coming home from school and being called into his "office"—the back room off our basement—and being told it was my turn to test these semiconductor things.

"Michael," my mom would call downstairs. "That's on the fringe of abuse. Our poor girls—you gotta give them a break." Mom would try to intervene so we could have somewhat of a normal after school life.

"But Katie, I need these tested. Promise, after this next box I won't bother the kids 'til the weekend," he would say in a pleading manner, giving me a hug as I continued testing these little metal mechanisms.

In the semiconductor world, if a certain percentage in a batch were bad, the entire batch would be tossed out, and I'm talking thousands. My dad had the foresight and his kids' fortitude to test each and every semiconductor in the bad batches, sort out the good ones, and sell them back to the company. Of course, this was all above board and the company my dad worked for at the time was thrilled to accommodate his efforts. Our long hours and bruised, tiny fingers raised over $50,000 in start-up money for our dad's company, Digimax, Inc.

In 1977, the company that would launch and support a more privileged life for our family opened its doors. Digimax, Inc. was an image processing company that developed real-time hardware and software products for the industrial, medical, military, and scientific markets.

The digital age was born, and my dad was at the forefront of this ginormous industry.

From a modest beginning to elite boarding schools and traveling abroad, my sisters and I never really noticed or even recognized the change in our lifestyle. It was just part of our lives, our journey. Mom and Dad were just that: mom and dad. Our baby brother was born in 1974, when all the 'good stuff' was starting to happen. Natalie, Grace, and I, being 12, 11 and 10 years older, were conveniently his built-in babysitters.

Noses pressed against the glass—looking back, that is exactly how it felt. We were introduced to and mingled with the elites of the world, but somehow, we were still not part of this circle. We were invited to participate, yet not fully accepted. From rooming with the DuPonts, dating the Prince of Holland, dining with the Dalai Lama, to racing in the infamous Italian Mille Miglia, our family was well versed in society. Traveling the globe was just part of our steps in life.

It wasn't anything to brag about; it just was. Digimax wasn't an overnight success. Our family worked long and hard. We helped our father build the business, and this equates in my book as a solid foundation.

Little by little, the sweetness of the successes was stripped away. Be it a wrong decision made or fate—I truly do not know. What I do know, it's not simply 20/20 hindsight. What echoes in my head is this scripture:

> *For it is by grace you have been saved through faith, and this not from yourselves; it is the gift of God, not by works, so that no one can boast. For we are God's workmanship, created in Christ Jesus to do good works which God prepared in advance as our way of life.*
>
> **Ephesians 2: 8-10**
> **(Scofield Study Bible, NIV)**

Did God build up and gift us an amazing life, then strip it away only in preparation for something more magnificent?

Growing up, we were not a God-fearing family. In fact, we were all over the board in respect to whether God was real or just a good idea. Like many, we went to church on Easter and Christmas. We had our Bibles, but how often were they opened, let alone read? In our eyes, life was what we made it. You work hard and the American Dream can become a reality.

We did work hard, we sacrificed, and we enjoyed some of the fruits of our labor—so why so temporary? Why such a brutal and devastating deconstruct of everything our family had worked so hard to achieve? Like a tornado coming in violently, swirling around, and piece by piece, breaking our future apart.

Drugs and alcohol were not the culprit—depression, despair and divorce were. Digimax opened its doors in 1977. It brought with it a pulse to life for many people for many years. In 2005, this beautiful ship went down, and with it, a flame of hope.

Our life during these years was like a magnificent roller coaster ride. The highs were exhilarating, and the lows devastating. Divorce seemed to be a common thread, and if I remember correctly, I started that trend. Nicholas and I went our separate ways in 1997; Grace and her husband, Sean, broke off a twenty- year marriage in 2007; my sister, Natalie, and her husband, Thomas, of eighteen years dissolved their union; and my mom and dad—forty years ended up in a divorce. Charlie was the only one in the family who escaped such a fate. He recognized the patterns of his older siblings and decided to wait in terms of getting involved in a serious relationship. He was the only one who got it right!

"Jess, life is so messed up," he would say. "I know what I want for myself, and I'm going to make certain I have it all together before I drag anyone else into my mess."

He continued, "Look what Dad put us all through. It was like we were his experiment. He tossed us around like a #$@&% salad whenever he liked. We weren't his family—Digimax was his family! We were just the extra stuff that seemed to get in the way most of the time. I didn't ask to be brought into this world. They did that, so…."

Yes, during the years that Digimax was a buzzword, life financially was secure; however, nothing is always as it seems behind closed doors. My parents had a very tumultuous relationship. In a strange way, they were good for one another, but let's just say that I too often was afraid of my dad, and I learned how to walk on eggshells at an early age. Mom was by no means silent or weak. She stood up to him (admirable), but many times she was the instigator of the storm. "There is more than one way to skin a cat," she would say.

We learned to be creative in order to keep the calm. Perspective? Imagine looking through broken glass. Beautiful, but fractured. The pieces might never again perfectly fit together as they once did.

Our flame of hope was redirected and, unfortunately, not upwards to God. Each of us was searching for our purpose in an already fallen and dark world.

I had just started dating Captain Ron. Ron had won over my mom and my brother, but other family members saw beyond the veil that clouded my judgement.

"What does she see in him?" I overheard Dad talking with a family friend, William Peters, on the phone. Unfortunately, Captain Ron overheard the conversation too. We had stopped by Dad's office earlier in the day to help with a move. When we walked in, he happened to be on the phone with his office door wide open. My father spoke in a very loud voice. It was hard NOT to hear what was being said (grimace face emoji). This scene would only add more fuel to the fire with his hatred and disrespect towards my family in years to come.

"Jessie could have anyone. She is a beautiful young woman, and she is with—I don't get it." He continued shaking his head. His tone of voice was frustrated and concerned.

I saw what I—or God—wanted me to see at the time; an adventurous, loving, and caring man who always put me first. He did not have deep pockets, but his experiences, his work ethic was admirable and, as a team, I saw a bright future.

Text to Ronald, August 22, 2018:

> I love you. But you do not see how your fears are directed at us and the intensity is like death. I have been scared of you for years…trying so hard to work with you - with the PTSD.

> It has nothing to do with the money. It has to do with your reactions directed at us. I am scared. The kids are scared. If you tru-

ly cared…you would not cut us off of all the finances. You took the SSI that belongs to the kids. Now you are trying to take my PFD?

A caring – NOT controlling husband would want to find out what went so terribly wrong and not use the fear tactic of lack of money to drive us back. If anything, you are driving us away even further.

Yes, I am upset. I have been upset for a very long time, but you just dismiss my feelings as being naïve.

PLEASE – Get help and stop trying to control us. Control does not equal love and protection!

The turbulence that I was accustomed to, the foundation of my youth, was a cakewalk to what I was enduring in my marriage. I feel as though I slipped through a crack and was pulled into some parallel universe, sort of like Neil Gaiman's *Coraline*. Initially, everything I dreamt of in my relationship seemed perfect, like a real-life fairytale. Ron was attentive to my needs, but was he? As I reflect, I can see a pattern. My nature was one to always accommodate someone else's needs before my own. Because life under the roof of my childhood was often stormy, I was determined to have a calm, healthy life with my husband and children, even if that meant doing backbends and cartwheels to achieve this. Was this a gift from God, part of my DNA, or survival behavior? I figured that if I just put my whole heart and soul into helping someone else, that should be enough for me, right? WRONG!

So, although my story started fifty-seven years ago when I was born, the part that is most important to share— that part was written over the last twenty-two years.

It starts off like a romance novel. Simple. Girl meets boy. Girl falls for boy. Boy tells girl he is going to marry her. Girl is puzzled but intrigued by boy's assertiveness. Girl marries boy, but NOT the wedding she dreamt of ...

"Oh well," is what I said then. My thought process was

that *if he is happy, then I am happy. If I put him first, then my dreams and desires will be addressed....Eventually?*

What happens when eventually never comes? What happens when the life that you dreamt of gets pushed further and further away? What happens when "dreaming" becomes a threat to your husband? What happens when you wake up one day and you realize that so much you worked for will NOT BE ALLOWED to happen? Allowed being the operative word.

Twenty-two years ago, I fell in love with a man who I thought was my everything. Twenty-two years ago, I was caught by a tormented soul who lured me deeper and deeper into HIS wants and needs. His ability to manipulate and control became my prison.

PLEASE remember, as strong as a relationship might seem, you only have to drop that 'glass' once for it to shatter.

"This family was not wired for normal; we are wired for AMAZING!" I was venting to my sister Natalie.

"All he wants to do is stay put and be safe. I feel like I am suffocating. What is life all about if you just survive? I need more, the kids need more." Both my sisters were amazing listeners. "I'm not being selfish, am I? I just know there is more out there for us, and I feel like he has put shackles around my ankles."

"Jess," Natalie responded to my tear-filled phone call. "It is time. You need to get an attorney and file for divorce. Ron will never change, and he will emotionally suffocate you, and the kids will be damaged goods. They will never know a healthy life."

Of course, I needed to vent, but didn't necessarily want to hear or take my sister's advice. My brain was hurting. The lack of money had been drilled into my soul as a given, even though I was able to manage a very nice life for my family. Money might have been tight, but it always seemed that when Ronald wanted something (Mustang, boat, guns), we could be creative and afford them.

It was this 'lack of money' theme that he would always use to rein me in. I do not know how and why I let this lie control me, but it did, and over the years, it did its damage.

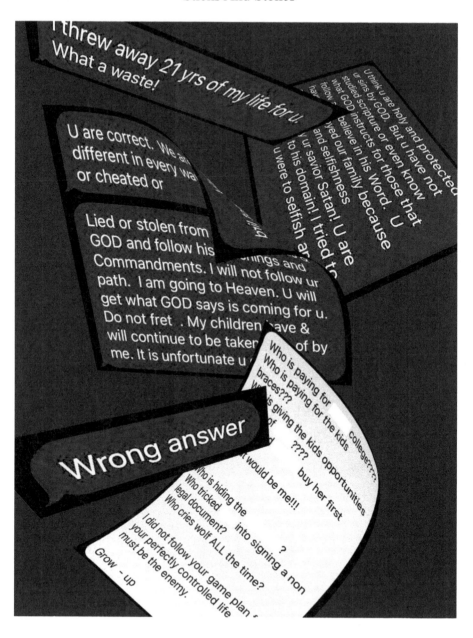

Text from Ron, February 26, 2022:

U think u are holy and protected in ur sins
by God. But u have not studied scripture
or even know what GOD instructs for
those that follow and believe his Word.
U have destroyed our family because of
ur vanity and selfishness promoted by ur
savior Satan! U are on your way to his
domain! I tried to help you but u were too
selfish and vain! I threw away 21 years of
my life for you. What a waste!

U are correct. We are totally different in
every way. I have not lied or cheated or
stolen from u. I love Jesus & God and
follow his teachings and Commandments.
I will not follow ur path. I am going to
Heaven. U will get what God says is coming for u. Do not fret. My children have
and will continue to be taken care of by

me. It is unfortunate u cannot!

My response:

Who is paying for Noah's college?

Who is paying for the kids' braces?

Who is giving the kids opportunities out-side of Ketchikan?

Who helped Sophia buy her first car?

Oh – that would be me!

Who is hiding the Shelby Mustang?

Who tricked our son into signing a non-le-gal document?

Who cries wolf ALL the time?

I did not follow your game plan for your perfectly controlled life so I must be the enemy.

Grow – up

His response:

Wrong answer

My purpose? God defines who I am:

One of you will say to me "Then why does God still blame us? For who is able to resist his will?" But who are you, a human being, to talk back to God? "Shall what is formed say to the one who formed it, 'Why did you make me like this?'" Does not the potter have the right to make out of the same lump of clay some pottery for special purposes and some for common use? What if God, although choosing to show his wrath and

make his power known, bore with great pa-
tience the objects of his wrath—prepared for
destruction? What if he did this to make the
riches of his glory known to the objects of his
mercy, whom he prepared in advance for glo-
ry— even us, whom he also called, not only
from the Jews but also from the Gentiles?

Romans 9: 19-24 (NIV)

RED FLAG

What had I done! My stomach was in knots, and if tears weren't rolling down my cheeks, I was using every ounce of energy to keep them from it. Everything I worked sooooo hard for, everything I dreamt about, was a farce. It was a joke. He never loved me or the kids. We were just an extension of him. We were his props.

Twenty-two years and I focused and held onto breadcrumbs. Those few amazing moments—were they really that amazing, or was I building them up to be something that they really weren't just so the kids and I could live a "Happily Ever After?"

GOD...what have I done?

The pain was REAL! The fear was REAL! The scars were REAL!

I was so tired. I was numb. What would I do now?

Starting over was very difficult … especially at fifty-four years old. BUT somehow, I knew that "God won't give me more than I can handle." I was desperately trying to convince myself of that.

GOD...I am on my knees! PLEASE HELP ME! I am truly broken. You shattered me!

My marriage was a nightmare and now You take my brother from me in the middle of it all? WHY? Charlie was not supposed to die. He was supposed to beat his cancer. He was only forty-four years old. He was an inspiration to us all. He has a beautiful young wife and a four-year-old daughter. They truly were a match made in heaven—a picture of perfection.

I just didn't get it!

I scribbled those words down only last month.

Not all marriages end up with an "And they lived happily ever after." In fact, the unfortunate truth is that the divorce rate is at an unprecedented high.

I so wish my story was a "happily ever after." I do not know the ending to this tale, but in that moment, as I wrote those words, it felt like my children and I were living in an inferno with no way out. I would not wish this on anyone.

God, I am scared. I am so very tired. I can't move forward without You. I am begging for You to hold my hand. Please carry me through this.

Red Flag

For my brother after his passing:

Charlie –You have been a shining star
since the day you were born. A son, a
brother, a husband, and a father. You challenged all, feared nothing and… put gray
hairs on many a head.

You had a thirst for life. You got it right
the first time… that is why God called you
home. He blessed us with your presence,
and through you He illustrated a joy that
can be obtained. Through you, God reminded us to always strive for your dreams!

Thank you for being who God created you
to be.

I am honored to be your big sister. I am
honored to call you my brother.

Love you forever and always,
Jess

March 2018

It was 6:15 in the morning. It was a school day. I was up getting the coffee on before waking the kids up. I received a text from my brother Charlie.

"Hey sis, it's bad news," is all that he said. I immediately picked up the phone and called him. The doctors got the preliminary test results back indicating the masses were malignant. I broke down in tears.

"Oh God! I'm coming down to see you," I exclaimed. "Can I come?"

"Yes, of course. I need all the support I can get," he answered. I could hear a nervous quiver in his voice, which is not like Charlie.

"I will be there this weekend," I stated.

"Great. Love you."

"Love you too, more than you can imagine." At this point, I was using every ounce of, I don't know what, to hold back the once-flowing tears just so I could muster up some strength for my brother.

I tried to clean myself up and keep myself composed while getting the kids off to school. After I dropped them off, I took a long walk with our dog, Stella. I walked along

Knudson Cove. Distracted and forlorn, I purposely kept my sunglasses on, as the tears just wouldn't stop.

Looking back, my tears were not only for my brother, but for the wrath that I was about to face when I would tell Ron that I needed to go spend time with Charlie. Unfortunately, I knew too well what his reaction would be… and supportive it was NOT.

I am so thankful that I chose to fight this battle. My gut told me that I needed to. If I had caved to Ron's wishes, I would not have spent that last summer with Charlie and have those amazing memories to cherish and hold on to. If I had caved and stayed home, Ron would have turned it around, twisting it somehow and telling me that he had never stopped me from going. Oh, and then I would only have myself to blame. He, Ron, did that ALL the time! He would make life so miserable, so unbearable, so icy cold. When I wanted to do something that was "seemingly" normal, but it wasn't something that he wanted to do, he would literally put us through HELL! And, after the fact, he would minimize the whole thing like it was nothing, or I was just way too sensitive.

"Jessie takes off whenever she likes," he would say in an accusing, defiant tone.

In nineteen years—in fact, from the time Ronald and I started dating in 1999—I have traveled without my Captain Ron seven times. Not seven times a year, but only seven individual trips over nineteen years. If his majesty wasn't keen on participating, he felt it was a waste of money or time or both. Forget about, "Hey babe, I don't want to go, but you go and have a good time." I never had his support or encouragement to do something that meant a lot to me.

2006 – Dad's Emergency Surgery

My first attempt to fly back East with the kids was crushed due to the extreme emotional outburst from Ron. This is the first I had seen in our relationship, and we had been together for almost seven years. It was so horrific that I called the airlines, canceled the trip, and because I was so shaken up, more like terrified by it, I lied! I told both the airlines and my family that Noah had an ear infection and that there was no way we could fly. We would have been traveling from Ketchikan, Alaska, to Boston. Noah was four and Sophia, two.

My father had a tumor on his lung. He was going in for surgery, but because of the positioning of the tumor, the doctors were going to perform a rather new procedure and access the mass through his back. I had received a call from my aunt letting me know the severity of my dad's condition.

When I first got the call, nothing was out of the ordinary in our relationship. I let Ron know that I needed to fly home, and he was a very caring and supportive husband. Although he wouldn't be able to travel with us, he was concerned about my dad's health and insisted that we go. Ron had just started a new management position and would be traveling up to Anchorage for work. The two trips coincided, so the timing seemed perfect.

It was the evening before we were supposed to leave that something went very wrong. Ron had come home from work, but he seemed out of sorts; annoyed somehow. When I asked him if everything was fine at work, he muttered something but didn't really answer. It was as if he was talking to someone else; someone in his head.

I walked back into the bedroom to continue packing. The babies and I had a 6:00 a.m. flight the next morning to Boston.

"My trip to Anchorage was canceled." He finally filled me in on a detail of what was possibly so annoying.

"Oh, I'm sorry, honey. Will you be okay while we're gone?" I tried to console him.

"You're NOT still going! What the @#$%! are you doing!" Ronald looked at me with dead eyes.

I was totally shocked. One, because he never spoke to me that way or used that tone. Two, because my dad was going into a surgery that he might not survive. Of course, we were still going. My heart started pounding nervously.

"Who is this man?" I thought to myself.

"Why the @#$%! do you need to see your father? He has never done anything for us!" Ron was spewing hate. This was NOT the man that I fell in love with.

"Ron," I said gently, trying to calm him down. "Come on, calm down. What's this all about? What's going on?"

"I'm going to be alone again. You are going to take the kids and never come back. It happened to me before and now you are going to do it, too!" He was talking at me and not making any sense.

I had never left Ron, nor had I ever thought about it. Up until this episode, our family was healthy.

"First Melissa, then Beth, and now YOU!" His head was reeling, and his ramblings were like a crazed man.

"Ron, I am not like your exes, nor do I ever intend to be. This is ridiculous. What really happened today?" I was trying to be stern in my questioning, trying to snap him out of whatever he was in.

"You "$@&%"! You are just like them," he snapped at me. He more than snapped at me. The foul language was being thrust at me as if I was his punching bag.

Now I was really scared. His body language was intense. He glared at me; his eyes with no soul behind them. Quietly, I left the bedroom and sat with the kids.

Ron's very bizarre episode lasted about three hours. When he went to bed, I could finally breathe, but I was still shaking like a leaf.

Oh God, what do I do? I need to see Dad. I wept.

I was confused, terrified, and overwhelmed. What just happened? I had to make a decision—a very difficult decision. There is a chance that my father might not survive his surgery, but my husband was suffering severely from a PTSD episode, and he was on the brink of falling down a very deep, dark rabbit hole.

I have no clue if I even slept that night. Our bags were packed, but—

The next morning, Ronald got up and got ready for work as if nothing had happened. He noticed that the kids and I were not ready for our trip. He didn't even ask if I had decided to still go or not. There were no words between us.

After he left, I collapsed in tears. My head was throbbing. It took a few hours, but I was able to collect my thoughts and phone my doctor. I needed to talk to someone. My family had enough on their plate with dad going into surgery. The last thing I wanted was for them to worry about me and the kids all the way in Alaska!

Tears take their toll, especially if you have been crying on and off for hours. My eyes were swollen, and I felt like a used-up dish rag thrown on the floor. Somehow, I kept my composure around the kids and only let the tears flow when they were napping or playing in their room. It is foolish to think that they didn't notice anything wrong, but I focused on calm—just keep calm.

"Ms. Millard," Dr. C received my message and made a point to call me back ASAP. "It sounds like your husband suffers from severe PTSD. And this is the first time you have seen this behavior?"

"Yes," I confirmed.

"He needs to see a psychiatrist immediately. Something triggered this, and it is not a healthy situation for you and the kids," Dr. C continued. "I'll make some calls and get him scheduled in."

"Thank you," I said with a sense of nervous relief

"But how do I tell him?" I asked. "After last night's—whatever that was—I don't want to push any buttons, if you know what I mean."

"Understood," Dr. Callahan responded with concern. "Where does your husband work? I can have Dr. Rand call him at work, try to intervene, and address the issue in a neutral location."

"Okay."

Ronald got home early that day. It was about 4:00 p.m. Not once did he bring up the outburst from the night before, nor the fact that the kids and I had not flown to Boston to see my father. Something just felt wrong, and I felt as though anything I might say would set him off again.

"What's wrong with you?" he asked in a rude, disgusted manner. "You look like @#$%!!"

Again, my nerves were frayed. I was clueless as to what was happening. Seven years and out of the blue—THIS? I did not know this person. I didn't want to know this person. I was terrified of this person.

It took about three days before I finally got back the Captain Ron I married. We rarely spoke of it, as he assured me that he would go to counseling on a regular basis. He never did apologize. What he did say was that he did not want to lose this family like he did the others.

Wow, if this is PTSD—what is tormenting him to put me in the line of fire? I thought to myself.

It would be another four years before the kids and I were once again subjected to Ron's irrational fears. Each new episode seemed to be triggered by the fact that we wanted or needed to travel outside of Ketchikan. Each new episode was more extreme and, unfortunately, the span between them grew closer and closer together.

We were now on that learning curve of walking on eggshells—adjusting our personalities to accommodate Ron.

Text that I sent to my husband, August 22, 2018:

> Ron,
>
> It got to the point that the kids and I were terrified of you. We are scared. Your PTSD is making us your enemy and we needed to leave before anyone was hurt. Please understand that this was the most difficult thing that I have ever done. I am asking that you get help. Let us have some time apart to heal. We are safe. Please! Please!

Red Flag

Please! You are so angry that you are directing it at us and scaring us.

Ronald's Response -

I have not gotten in any fights, been arrested, passed out drunk in the street, slept with prostitutes, gambled, stayed away for days, disappeared, done drugs. Loved you and the kids more than life. I have been the best I could be and that is more than anyone you know or ever will.

Never lied, cheated stole or fabricated #$@&! to fool you. Ever. I always do what I say and say what I do. How can that scare you?
I just don't understand why you are afraid.
I have never been violent with any of you.
Please come home.

Is God telling you to leave your husband

and destroy your family or are you being

manipulated by Satan?

You have everything – everything u and

the kids own is here. What are you think-

ing?

U are living amongst the most evil of hu-

mans and u claim to be afraid of me?

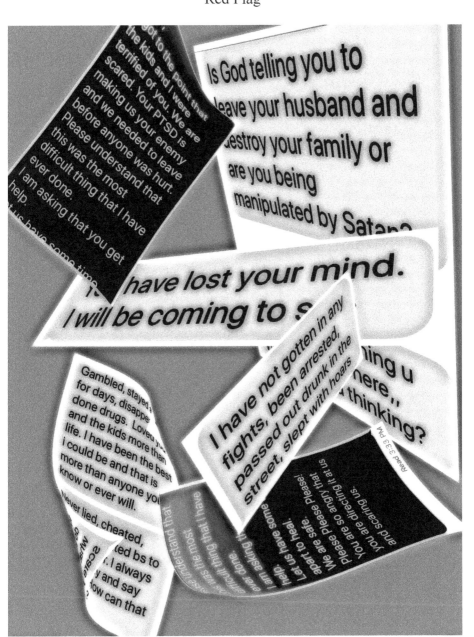

KNIGHT IN SHINING ARMOR

According to Webster's Dictionary, a relationship is defined as the way in which two or more people or group regard and behave towards each other. The definition of marriage goes one step further, it is a formal union and social and legal contract between two individuals that unites their lives legally, economically, and emotionally.

It was the summer of 1997. A chapter in my life was closing. I had been in a relationship with a very talented photographer for a decade. We dated for seven years and were married for three. We met in what seemed to be a very small circle of an industry I had been working in—fashion and advertising. I was a fashion model, and he was … you guessed it … a photographer. Perfect match? Yes, and no. Nicholas was sixteen years my senior. He was my BEST friend and, as a team, we worked together seamlessly. Initially, I was one of the models he would photograph on a regular basis; however, as our time spent together grew, I found myself investing in our relationship both financially and emotionally.

Prior to meeting Nicholas, I had what many thought to be a very glamorous life. At the age of fourteen, I had been discovered by one of Eileen Ford's scouts. Yes, the very same, Eileen Ford of Ford Modeling Agency in New York City. This part of my life could be a novel in its own right, but suffice it to say, I was sent to Paris, and one summer, it blossomed into a twenty-year career. Although I did not become a household name in the industry, work was steady, especially since the German catalogs seemed to love my look. I worked abroad for about ten years, only coming home for the holidays. Home at the time was Boston. Yup—good 'ole *Bean Town*. While visiting family, I would often pick up a few modeling assignments in the local market, thus how I met my first husband.

I have been married twice, and both ended up broken! The failed marriages too often tormented me. I am the common denominator in both. It must be me! What am I doing wrong? Am I selfish? Am I unrealistic in what I want, or maybe, I'm plain just not good enough?

Looking back at my relationship with my first husband and comparing it to my current marriage, I did notice a pattern. Although Nicholas and Ron were very different, they had underlying similarities that attracted me to them. Both partners were sixteen years my senior. Both partners had a creative or adventurous nature. Both partners had a dedication and work ethic that was admirable. Both partners had faced financial difficulties—bankruptcy. AND—highlighting AND—both partners NEEDED the attention of others to prop themselves up.

"SUPPORT! I can do that. I don't mind helping others." I was always eager to jump in and help. "After all, isn't that what a friend or caring partner does?" Shockingly, I realized that I wanted to help "FIX" something that was missing in their lives, or so I thought.

Unfortunately, this is where I had gone wrong. A healthy relationship is about giving, yes; however, it is a two-way street. If all one partner does is give, then he or she will eventually run dry. A healthy relationship also has and respects boundaries. I, unfortunately, rarely put up any boundaries. I naïvely assumed that "the love of my life" would eventually reciprocate. I would pour my heart, soul, and finances into helping them fuel their dreams while at the same time putting mine on the back burner.

To his credit, Nick was an amazing artist and a decent human being. I have many more fond memories than not. Our marriage began to crumble when I wanted to start a family. We were both passionate about the work we did together, but our relationship stalled there. The intimacy was lacking. Nicholas thrived in the creative process, and I loved being a part of that, but outside of the studio, our common interests started to fall flat. Looking back, Nicholas and I should have never married.

To be honest, I can't blame Nick. Wait! Yes, I can—it's just that I was so eager to give and to please. I led myself down a dark path. And I will take total responsibility for that, but he did not have to exploit my kindness and trust. He did not have to "dangle that proverbial carrot" for all those years.

"UHGGGGG." I felt like Rapunzel in the Disney film *Tangled.*

So, marriage one ended. I was thirty-three years old and at a place in my life that I desperately wanted to start a family. That motherly instinct / time clock was ticking, my modeling career was coming to a close and, I hate to admit this, my financial situation was no longer healthy, having invested in the wrong person.

"Hey sis, time to come home for a bit," my brother, Charlie—on the phone at that time, was insistent and wouldn't take no for an answer. Charlie was ten years younger than me and my biggest fan. He was also Mr. Adventurous himself. "The beach will be good for you and

I'm sure Mom and Dad won't mind forking over some dough. What are parents good for, anyway?"

"I know they will. It's just that I feel like a fool."

Our parents had a lovely home on Cape Cod. It would always be our retreat away from the Big Apple. Charlie had been living with former college buddies on the upper East Side, while Nicholas and I had a small studio on the upper West Side. With the marriage over, my brother was encouraging me to step away from the industry for a bit. He dared me to enjoy life outside of the rigors of dieting and staying out of the sun.

"Come on! How 'bout sailing again? We can head up tomorrow. You drive," he grinned from ear to ear.

He had this smile; this way about him—dang; I am soooo lucky to be his sister. Charlie talked about sailing, but he sold my Sunfish without my even knowing AND kept the money (eyes roll) and, of course, he wanted a ride! I had kept my car in the city—he had been partying all night, so Big Sis would be his five-hour taxi ride home (again, eyes roll). 'Gotta love baby brothers! As mischievous, adventurous, and wonderfully crazy as Charlie was, I knew his heart was in the right place and he always had my back.

Knight in Shining Armor

Text Ron sent to our daughter, Sophia, February 2022:

> I have ur mothers income IRS records
> since she was 16. She made no money
> until she married me. Ur mom told us all
> lies! Her modeling income was less than
> what u make a month as a cookie assem-
> bler. She is telling us all lies!

The next couple of years I spent trying to reinvent myself. My career as a model had slowed down to a crawl. The industry was changing, and my look was no longer in demand. Nicholas and I had decided to share the studio in New York City on an alternating basis while I worked at establishing a new career. My skill set in the photography and production arena was sound, so I tried my hand at that.

Any change in life is challenging, especially when you are leaving a partnership and forced to start over. When I was with Nicholas, my career as a fashion model flowed seamlessly into my role as studio manager, partner, and wife. Now that the marriage was over, working together seemed awkward and, as I was no longer in the supportive role, I felt vulnerable. I also had that yearning to start a family.

October 1999

During this 'gap,' my life was by no means dull. I had literally traveled around the globe as a photographer's assistant, dined with the Dalai Lama, studied Kabala, and even reconnected with a former boyfriend who was into auto sports. Not dull, but not complete either. I felt fractured, like something was missing. The pieces of my life's puzzle weren't fitting together smoothly like I thought they should or had in the past.

Have you ever had an epiphany? That moment when you suddenly feel that you understand something. That *Aha* moment? When life felt confusing and extremely unsettled, I had an epiphany. I woke up from a dream at three o'clock in the morning and just knew that I was supposed to travel to Hawaii! Yeah right—you are thinking. Everyone "dreams" of a trip to that tropical paradise. Seriously, mine was not because of a mere wish. I was a seasoned traveler and spent many years traveling to spectacular places. Interestingly enough, Hawaii was never one of those destinations.

Crazy as this might seem, with life upside down and finances very, very, very tight, I followed my gut and—booked an extended trip to our fiftieth state.

"Sis, hey, I'll join you if I find the time." Charlie was

keen on my upcoming spontaneous adventure. "Who knows, maybe you'll stay and then I'll have a palm tree to crash under." He was quite the wise guy.

"For you—anything." I retorted.

"Seriously though," he continued, "it'll be good for you. Clear your head and help you get back on track—you know—your old self."

"I suppose you're right." I responded. "You sure I'm not just being crazy and running away?"

"YOU?" Charlie exclaimed. "You are the most responsible and safe person any of us have ever known. It's time you shake things up a bit—have a little FUN—RELAX."

My baby brother was right. I was very conservative in my choices. Investing in myself and having FUN wasn't a high priority on my list.

I hesitantly shared my plans with my family and even my ex, Nick. Surprisingly, all were encouraging and supportive. Nicholas even booked me as his photo assistant for an advertising campaign, so I would have some extra cash for the trip. See, he is a good guy at heart—BUT— what did that say about me? Either I was truly prudish in my ways, and they wanted to break my mold, or they were trying to get rid of me? I'll go with – hmmm –

OK, off I went. A single, 35-year-old woman books a six-week trip to Maui, HI to—find a new life, and maybe meet my future husband?

September 9th I was on a flight to the Valley Island. Taking a deep breath, I had this weird feeling my life story would change completely.

Oh, God! What am I doing?

Maui is not called the Valley Island for nothing. It is breathtakingly exquisite! The air wraps a welcoming, warm, fragrant blanket around you. I was in paradise! My plans were to do absolutely NOTHING! Sleep under a palm tree, take long walks on the alluring, white, sandy beaches, maybe learn how to scuba dive. I promised myself not to have an agenda, just to explore and enjoy one day at a time.

Little did I know, doing absolutely nothing can get a bit humdrum, monotonous, mundane—you get the picture. I was used to always being busy. When I finally STOPPED, I didn't know what to do with myself. I felt empty and alone. That ugly shadow of vulnerability had followed me to this tropical paradise.

"Local artist seeking an assistant," the paper on the community board said.

I tore off one of the tabs with a phone number on it. *Why not look for work? It will be a good distraction.* I thought to myself. I really did not know the definition of downtime and I was desperately trying to fill a void in my life.

Like the roads on this magnificent volcanic island, my time spent on Maui took many twists and turns. I was captivated by the island's splendor; however, that emptiness manifesting inside of me was preventing me from truly experiencing its magnificence. I was present, yet at the same time lost in thoughts of being at a different place in my life.

I filled my days and nights with touristy distractions, as well as "assisting" my new artist friend to promote and sell her paintings. Oh, that advertisement on the community board? That "job" was an unpaid position as an artist's assistant (insert shrugged shoulders emoji). Denise was an immensely talented artist; however, she had this very attractive and persuasive way about her. Before I knew it, I was following her around the island, helping her set up for shows. I didn't mind. I had made a new friend and was back in a supportive role.

Familiarity. When something is familiar, it can feel comforting and secure, even if what is familiar isn't necessarily healthy. I was familiar with jumping in and helping others out, even if that meant putting my dreams on hold. I was back in my comfort zone. This wasn't necessarily unhealthy, but it certainly wasn't productive if I wanted to move towards my goals. Call it a safe detour.

It was a week before my stay on Maui was about to end. A friend of Denise's was asking me if I had experienced the Na Pali Coast.

"The what?" I asked, feeling a bit stupid.

"Obviously you haven't—BUT you must before you leave!" Freddie exclaimed. "It is the most spectacular coastline on the planet. Hollywood even films there."

"Boat tour, helicopter tour?" I was trying to get a feel of how I could experience this Na Pali Coast.

"Deep Blue Adventures!" he excitedly replied.

Let me back up. Fred was more like an acquaintance of Denise rather than a friend. He was a nice fellow but a bit too eager, if you know what I mean? He would randomly show up at the venues we were at and "hang around."

"Freddie? He's harmless. But don't be surprised if he asks you to be his girl. That's his thing. He likes to woo the howlie girls who are on vacation. He thinks he's hoping to land himself a sugar momma." Denise shook her head in disapproval.

"Jess," Denise continued. "I think you should go."

I was hoping that Denise would have my back—jump in and shoo him away—BUT instead she encouraged me to go! And to make it even more awkward, right in front of him.

"Uh—so where is this Deep Blue Adventures and how much does it cost?" I was trying to plant a seed to kindly decline Fred's invitation.

"Ma'alaea Harbor, and I am one of the crew, so the trip is complimentary for you," he pleadingly insisted.

"Thank you so much, Freddie, but I don't think I will be able to." I tried to back myself out of a corner.

"Jess, it is spectacular and even more so if the trip is comped for you." My artist friend was NOT helping.

"Then you come too," I suggested.

"Can't," she replied.

"Can't or won't?" I muttered under my breath.

Fred jumped in, noticing that there was ever the slightest chance I would accept his offer. "I'll pick you up at 8:30 a.m."

"No, no, that's not necessary," I reacted. "I'll meet you at the dock."

God forbid I give this guy the wrong impression PLUS get stuck with him driving. Ma'alaea was over an hour away from the cottage I was renting.

"So, you'll go with me?" Fred was practically panting like a little puppy.

"I'll only go with you as a guest. Freddie, you are a sweet guy, but I'm NOT your girlfriend!" I reminded him profusely.

"You might just change your mind after tomorrow," he said with a crocodile grin on his face.

Fred just had to get the last word in—what was I getting myself into?

October 10, 1999

Okay Lord, I hope this is worth it!"

I remember it like yesterday. It was a Monday morning—Columbus Day, to be exact. I jumped in my car and drove from my beachside bungalow to Ma'alaea Harbor. It was a winsome drive along the coast and going through the tunnel of trees was filmic. The beauty this island displayed was finally starting grow on me—yeah, now that I was about to leave. The Deep Blue trimaran tour set sail at 11:00 a.m. I pulled into the dusty parking lot at Ma'alaea Harbor thirty minutes prior. I was secretly hoping to miss Fred and NOT step aboard, but no such luck. Denise's friend saw me and ran over to the car.

"You made it!" Freddie energetically greeted me. "Promise, you'll have a fabulous time."

I walked with Fred to where the vessel is docked.

"Hey, guys," he announced to the crew, "this is my girlfriend, Jessica, I was telling you all about."

"Your what?" I elbowed him with an agitated smile. "No, just a friend being demoted to acquaintance if he keeps this up."

I made certain to correct my relationship status and inform the crew of that. I was not in the mood to play games and really didn't care if he uninvited me—kicked me off the tour.

Okay, this part of my story gets a bit bizarre. It even made my head spin. So, I had NO CLUE what tall tales Mr. Freddie had been spreading. But when I was waiting to board the Deep Blue, Mark, another crew member, came over and asked me if I really was Freddie's girlfriend.

"NO!" I said emphatically. "What has he been telling you all?"

"Only that he is madly in love with you," Mark informed me as he was heading back to the boat.

"Great! Just great," I sighed. "Maybe this is a bad idea after all."

I mentioned to Mark that I did not appreciate the rumors that Fred had been spreading, so—me and the Na Pali Coast could be "two ships passing in the night."

"Please don't go. I'm sorry. I promise to be good. I want you to at least enjoy the Na Pali," Freddie pleaded with me as I was returning to my car.

"Well, okay," I hesitantly replied. "Seriously though, Fred, I am in no mood for rumors or drama. You promise?"

We headed over to the trimaran. There were about forty passengers on this voyage. I filtered myself in the line of eager tourists. I seemed to be the only single person, but then again, most 'normal' folks come to a romantic tropical paradise island with their someone special. As I was embarking on the vessel, the captain—a ruggedly handsome guy sort of like a Crocodile Dundee—was welcoming each guest aboard.

"You're NOT Freddie's girlfriend, are you?" he inquired as he helped me step from the dock onto the boat.

"FRIEND—only friend." Again, correcting the rumor the crewmember had been spreading.

Okay, this is going to sound totally strange and spontaneous, but as he was holding my hand, assisting me onboard, Captain Ron paused and didn't let me go. He just looked at me and then announced: "I'm going to marry you!" confirming this thought he had mustered up in his mind.

"Uh—excuse me? We don't even know one another!" I responded with a very confused look.

"Oh, we will!" he said in a curiously resolute manner.

Text from Ronald, January 2022:

> Time to sell everything gypsy!
>
> I will now tell our children about what
>
> Freddie told me about having sex with you
>
> on the beach at ke alia before I met you on
>
> the ocean dolphin! And if they don't be-
>
> lieve me my family will continue the nasty
>
> details for years after my death. U are a liar

and a cheat and have destroyed my entire life that was planned for us and our children. U are evil and GOD will not allow u into Heaven!

RUNNER!

You taught them to be just like u (throw up emoji)

GILDED CAGE

Ronald and I had a healthy relationship, or so I thought. We met and started dating in October 1999 and we did not get married until April 2001. Initially, our relationship was long distance as I had met my Captain Ron while visiting the Valley Isle of Maui, and I resided in Boston. After we met, he dropped many hints for me to abandon my old life and just stay in paradise with him, but I was being the responsible one and declined with a hopeful smile.

"If we are meant to be, the magic of Maui will be with us no matter where we are." I snuggled into his arms and gave him a kiss. "I need to know it is you that I am absolutely nuts about, and not this picture-perfect place."

Ron was living aboard his 48' catamaran. The week we spent together before I had to leave was none less than heaven.

Wrapping his arms around me, he smiled and agreed. "Distance will tell the truth. Either our hearts will grow fonder or fade apart."

I flew back East on October 30, 1999. I had a lot on my plate when I got home. Catching up on what my next phase in life would look like after being away for six weeks wasn't the smoothest transition.

Maybe I shouldn't have bailed and just stayed, I dreamily thought to myself. *It was so perfect; he was so perfect.*

There definitely was an attraction between us. After I left, we called one another all the time.

"Who are you talking to?" asked my mom.

Ron had called yet again. Probably the fourth time that day. With each call, my body language would become more fluid, happier, if that makes any sense. We were flirting over the phone. My mom was beyond thrilled to see me in this state.

"I've never seen Jessie look so healthy!" mom quietly exclaimed to her friend Nan. "Who are you talking to again?" she was teasingly prying to find out if I had a new beau.

"Captain Ron," I responded, rolling my eyes as if she didn't know.

"Oh, and he's a captain!" she was encouragingly jabbing me. "Well, tell your captain that your mother says, Aloha."

I remember it being an exhilarating day! I was staying with my mom at the Cape house. Mom's best friend, Nan, was over (oh, those two—watch out, world, when they get together). Ronald and I engaged in many flirtatious phone calls and the next thing I knew, my mom was grabbing the phone away from me.

"Captain Ron, you need to come out for a visit. As Jessica's mother, I insist, and you will be my guest."

"Mom," I grabbed the phone back.

"Is that a real invite?" Ron asked.

"Let me call you back," I said, and ended the call.

Mom and Nan were thrilled that they had intervened.

"What? YOU, sweetheart, are beaming! What was your mum supposed to do?" Nan gave my mom a 'high five.'

On November 10, 1999, Captain Ron made his way from Maui, Hawaii, to Boston. When I picked him up at the airport, my heart was pounding. Approaching me was this lean, ruggedly handsome man. It was like a scene in a romantic Hollywood film.

Needless to say, not only did I really, really, like him; when I introduced Captain Ron to my mom and brother, he captivated them, too. He seemed to enchant everyone he spoke to. His lifetime of adventures and stories were beyond anyone's imagination, and they were all true. He was like Indiana Jones, Crocodile Dundee, and Quinn Harris (*Six Days Seven Nights*) all rolled into one. The best part is, Captain Ron came to see me.

His initial ten-day visit turned into a full-on life together.

Ronald's Text, August 22, 2018:

> All the years, things, and places we have been and done. It was fun. We would still be doing but we had to stop and provide a safe and nurturing place for the kids. That is what you told me you wanted when we first met. It took many years and hard times, but we finally put it together. Why would you want to blow it up? I gave you what I promised. I don't want to die a lonely unhappy old man.

In November 2005, we moved from Maui, Hawaii, to Ketchikan, Alaska, when Ronald was offered a lead management position at a large boating manufacturing company. The kids were little. Sophia was eighteen months and Noah was a toddler at three and a half years old. Ketchikan is remote, but incredibly charming. The island community was something like one would imagine in a Hallmark film.

Everyone was incredibly supportive, but at the same time, knew everybody else's business. It was the perfect place to settle and raise our two children.

In February 2007, we bought our first home together—a beautiful contemporary oceanfront house, with a spectacular view of the mountains.

Except for that very odd, isolated episode Ronald had a year prior, life was healthy, not perfect by any means—but healthy. My husband's work transitioned from him being a manager at the shipyard to becoming the general manager of an exclusive Sport Fishing Lodge. He was in his element, and I was in mine. After all, I had a loving, hardworking husband and two beautiful children.

What I did not see in my crystal ball was that there was a very dark cloud looming on the sidelines.

I'm not certain if living remote can help or hinder someone suffering from PTSD. The beauty of Alaska is raw and exquisitely breathtaking, but the solitude has its demons. I was very busy with raising the kids and working alongside Ron. My life was good, for the most part. We had a beautiful home, and I was not shy in becoming a part of the community, participating in fundraisers, school projects, and the like.

Money, or the lack thereof, can be stressful for any relationship. Ronald and I both worked hard in and out of the home. While my Captain Ron was managing the lodge, I wore many hats: wife, mom, my husband's assistant, freelance photographer, and skincare representative for an online company. Ron loved that I was versatile and willing to work alongside him. What I started to become aware of was that he wasn't the most supportive when I worked on my own projects. Initially, I chalked it up to his caring and that he was concerned that I didn't burn myself out. But as time went by, there was a definite animosity towards me making an income of my own. This did not make any sense to me. If finances were tight and I could help contribute, why the resentment?

2010 – NuSkin Ruby Trip

I had been a representative for the company, NuSkin, for about a year. With all my finesse and hard work, I had elevated to the Ruby Level. With this came the perk of an all-expense paid trip to company headquarters in Utah. It was a four-day trip to a beautiful spa resort.

Did I mention "ALL EXPENSES PAID" for two? Of course, when I received the call from my supervisor that I had been awarded the trip, I accepted without hesitation.

"Hey babe," I said teasingly. "Guess what you and I are doing in two weeks?"

Ron just looked at me as he walked by.

"Don't you wanna know where we're off to?"

"Jess, what are you talking about?" he said in a somewhat irritated voice.

"Seriously, Ron, we're going to Utah. I have been awarded the Ruby trip. All expenses paid for you and me," I continued.

"You didn't accept it, did you?" he asked.

"Of course, I did. Why?"

"There is no way we are going. Why the #$@&! would

I want to go on a trip like that? What, spend four days with 'fufu' men and women who sell vitamins? And who will watch the kids? The plane goes down and we leave them as orphans. Are you insane?" He kept rambling on about how out of touch I was with reality, how selfish and inconsiderate I was, and how dangerous traveling would be. After all, in his mind, the lower 48 was a war zone.

"Kelly has offered to watch the kids and those 'fufu' men and women—you must be referring to your own wife," I retorted. I didn't want to start an argument, but I was feeling that uncomfortable insanity emerging. I would get brief glimpses of it from time to time, but for the most part, Ron was able to keep it at bay.

The conversation escalated into a one-sided verbal assault towards me and my behavior. How dare I make any plans outside of his comfort zone? How dare I be independent?

He assumed I would back down as I had years prior, but this time I had the courage to call his bluff.

"You're not actually thinking of going?" Ronald with disgust.

I didn't answer him. What I did do was instead invite a girlfriend of mine to join me. When the plans were changed, I informed him that he and the kids would have a fabulous long weekend together while Mommy traveled.

This did not go over well at all. That is an understatement! My announcement triggered a violently emotional response. Ron was not physically violent towards us, but the verbal onslaught was like walking a very fine line which sent us all into therapy for the next week.

With the support and encouragement of my therapist and friends, I did go on the trip with my friend Allie. Ron and the kids were fine without me for four days. The plane did not crash, and I did return home.

Unfortunately, the pattern of these triggers was starting to emerge, as well as the intensity of them. What I need to explain is that the triggers ONLY EVER HAPPENED when it involved something that meant something to me and the kids. If it was for or about Ron—NO PROBLEM!

2014 – America's Got Talent

Our daughter, Sophia, was invited to audition in front of the judges for America's Got Talent. Our little town of Ketchikan put on fundraisers so we could take her back East for the live audition. Ron did not want any part of this. He did not want our daughter to audition, even though she poured her little heart and soul out preparing for it. With the support of family and friends and with the financial support from the folks in Ketchikan, I took Noah and Sophie back East for her audition. We were gone for six days.

2014 – Family Reunion

My brother and his new wife, Andrea, had just given birth to their daughter, Lynn. My mother invited our entire family, yes, this included Ron, out to California so we could all be together. My mother also offered to pay for our entire trip, as she knew money could be an issue. I accepted. Ron was more than upset. He was beyond upset. The fact that I accepted to go, wanted to go, was maddening to him. I pressed forward and was determined to have some normalcy in my life. Initially, we (mom and I) decided just Sophie and I should come as Noah had a difficult time around newborns. This seemed to ease the stress of the upcoming trip until Ron saw the dates for our flight.

"Jessica, how long are you going to be gone?" he asked in an agitated manner.

"Thirteen days. We fly out on the Monday and return on…" My nerves were consuming me.

"You don't need to be gone that long. I LOVE how you

just love to jump and leave your family!" He was enraged.

"I'm not flying all the way to California for a weekend. It's summer. It's vacation. You should come with us. You are invited," I quietly stated.

"What the #$@&%! do I want to go to San Francisco for? Why the #$@&%! would I want to spend time with YOUR family? They mean nothing to me." Ron would always find ways to put my family down.

Things got bad at home. Ron told me that if I insisted on taking this trip, he would file for divorce. Also, my husband was becoming so unstable that Dr. Ward, Ron's psychiatrist, and I agreed I'd best bring Noah with me as well.

One night, because Ronald couldn't "get to me," he stooped really low. He threatened our daughter, Sophie. He told her that if she went on the family reunion trip, he was going to give her dog away! Sophe was only ten years old. She was devastated. I was devastated. In my pajamas, I took both children and our dog, Stella, and left for the night. We stayed with a dear friend. Phone calls and many, many tears to family members were to follow.

The kids and I made the family reunion. Being with family was beyond needed. We had a restful and fun time.

Unfortunately, with incident. Ron would call, threatening to have the FBI arrest me. Determined to make my marriage work and help Ronald through his PTSD and insecurities, the children and I returned home as originally planned.

2015 – Biopsy

I had to fly down to Seattle for an ultrasound-guided biopsy. It was a simple procedure and an overnight stay. Our little community did not have the necessary modern medical equipment; however, my husband was not supportive of my going. He would have rather have me scared by the old techniques than fly down. I gave him a cold stare.

"We don't have the money," he complained.

"So, I'm supposed to subject myself to a knife and have scar tissue?" I just shook my head.

I called my sister, and she immediately wired me funds for the airfare.

2015 – Nonmalignant Tumor

The biopsy results came back inconclusive. After several phone consultations and a meeting with my primary care physician, we agreed it would be safer to have the mass removed. It was located next to my left breast under the armpit area. The concern was if there was a malignancy, and it was near the lymph—well, best to be safe than sorry.

It was the beginning of summer, and Sophie asked if she could join me. We would be staying with Ron's sister, Diane. We planned to be in Washington for ten days. We gave ourselves enough time for the surgery, recovery, and, hopefully, clean results. The surgery went really well and after four days, the results came back negative. Instead of Ronald being relieved and encouraging Sophia and me to relax now and enjoy time in the Seattle area, he insisted that we come straight home. Don't fret, my daughter and I stayed the entire ten days.

2018 – Charlie's Cancer

On March 31, 2018, Sophia and I flew to San Francisco to spend time with my brother. We were there for the initial investigation of what kind and how advanced his cancer was. Making this trip was another huge trigger, setting off a week of agony in our home. My husband tried every manipulative strategy to keep us from going. From silent treatments, financial threats, dead cold stares, to violent outbursts that sent the kids and me into hiding.

On the morning of our flight, with it being Easter weekend, I had the house completely cleaned, the grocery shopping done, and even had a stew simmering in the oven for Ron and Noah. It was getting time for Sophe and me to head to the airport. Ronald was supposed to take us, but he went one step further; this time, he refused to get out of bed complaining of a stomachache.

I think I was becoming numb to his behavior. This time, I simply called my friend Lee.

"Hey sweetie, any chance you could drive us to the airport?" I asked.

"He's not going to take you, is he?" She knew his patterns of control.

"Nope."

"I'll be there in twenty. Does that work?" Lee asked.

"Perfect! See you soon. Love you!"

I was so appreciative of my friends and their support. I really tried not to get them involved, but as the episodes and the intensity of his reactions increased, my close-knit friend circle was holding my family in their daily prayers and was now stepping in.

We spent nine days with Charlie, Andrea, and Lynn. Time I now know I will NEVER get back!

August 2, 2018 – ICU

Charlie was being rushed to the hospital with trouble breathing. It was time for the family to step in and help out more and more. Ronald did not think it necessary, nor my place, to go.

"Charlie is my brother!" I inserted my stance.

"You are crazy. You would throw away this family just to 'help out?'" He actually thought he was convincing me to make a choice. "That is why they have places like hospice."

Of course, I would not listen to him anymore. I booked a flight and went down, leaving my two children behind. That very night, the monster let loose. Ronald became so unhinged and angry at the thought of me merely taking a taxi to my brother's house; I was fearful for the safety of my children.

August 19, 2018 – The GREAT ESCAPE

Never to return!

Seven times. Seven times in nineteen years. Not seven times a month. Not seven times a year. Seven times in NINETEEN years. But according to Ron, I took off whenever I felt like it!

Ronald:

> Liar and betrayal as foreseen in the bible. You will always be known as a liar and [expletive] throughout history of my family and God. (Ron would call me vile names – this being the other word for prostitute.)

Sheila, Ronald's sister:

> Seriously Jessica?
>
> All in God's time huh?
>
> More like, let's leave and see how bad

I can screw him, he was such a bad husband and father. What the heck happened
to you? Take Sophie baby and go to Europe
like she wants to do. Let Noah stay with
his father and go back to school. Amazing
how much she dislikes her father. He took
up too much of your time I guess. You have
totally blown me away. My brother doesn't
deserve this, and you know it. You are not
the Jessica I knew.

As I did not react nor respond to Sheila's insulting text
message, Sheila writes another message a couple days later:

Jessica I'm sorry that I have been so rude
and spiteful to you. You are one of the
sweetest and sincere people I have ever
known. I have cried and I have prayed a lot
this past week. I know my brother is devastated and is seeing his shrink as often as
possible. He had no idea how he was com-

ing across to you and the children. Money is almost always the nucleus of problems in a marriage. After talking to him at length every day, I know that is where most of his anxiety comes from. Also added in there is the fact that he feels he cannot protect ya'll if you move to a larger city. We are trying to work through that. I'm especially sorry for saying you and Sophia should just go to Europe. You know me well enough to know my mouth needs to remain closed when I'm emotional. Ronnie misses ya'll so much and is like a lost child without you. I understand finally about your need to heal. I also think that he needed this wakeup call. I pray that given some time, you will be able to forgive him and me. I am encouraging him to stop drinking again and work on facing your problems together. You have been a steadying force in his life and mine, actually. We both love you bigly … please forgive me for letting my voice overload my reasoning. I love you like a sister. I don't want to face the fact that you may not want to be with him anymore. (praying emoji, sad emoji, head down emoji).

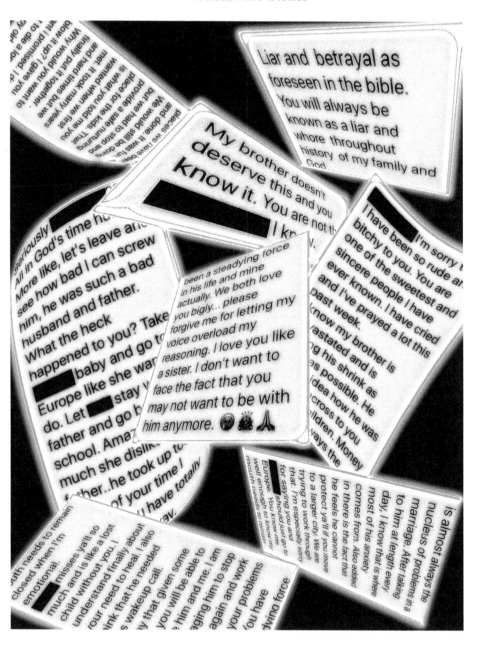

UNHINGED

WORDS—more so—descriptive words.

I let a friend of mine read a few chapters of my manuscript the other day as I continue (in an attempt) to put down on the written page the hell that my kids and I not only became accustomed to but lived through for so many years.

His response was encouraging, but at the same time a disconnect.

"Jess, I need to see more. I mean, you need to develop the details. I want to know what that room looked like. I want to smell the surroundings." His literacy advice came pouring in.

As I listened seriously with an open mind, my stomach turned. He doesn't get how hard this is to relive. He doesn't understand that each memory opens a wound that crushes me. Sometimes I find myself staring at the screen, hearing the tormenting insults being hurled at me, and then that protective wall comes up. I go numb like a haze rushing in— in disbelief that my life ever went down this road.

Sticks and Stones is NOT about the flowery wallpaper in the bathroom or the aroma of a stew sizzling in the oven. It's not about the surroundings because this is not a fantastic mystery or fanciful novel. This is about a world that slowly consumed my self-worth and that of my children. This is about falling in love with a man (monster) who ultimately did not have our best interest at heart—only his own.

"Ron, we are not connected at the hip, for God's sake!" I was defensively responding to something.

"We better the #$@&%! be," he continued, "otherwise, why the #$@&%! did I ever marry you?"

That was it. I was not his equal, nor a loving partner. I was an appendage. My husband thought of me as an extension of himself, or even lower than that, his property.

That thought suffocated me. I felt the walls closing in even faster than before.

It didn't matter if I was sitting in a coffee shop with friends, visiting with family in California, or crying in that corner of my kitchen, because as long as I was his wife, I would never have autonomy. I would always feel the psychological pressure he used to control me.

What needs to be developed and revealed is how the

slow, methodical twists and turns—the calculated manipulation over months and years beat me down to a scared, frail, shell of a person.

God woke me up!

My sister once told me this: throw a frog in a pot of boiling water and what does it do? Well, it jumps out! You put that very same frog in a lukewarm bath of water and ever so slowly turn up the heat—that frog falls asleep and withers away.

Ronald, over the years, had been lulling us to sleep, and as we withered into compliance, the shackles were slapped on. When we did wake up, it was too late—well, almost. My son was suicidal; my daughter was going down that same dark path with anxiety and deep depression, and I held the key. If I didn't do SOMETHING—forget that—I had to do something, and that is when I continually cried out to God!

There was NEVER any physical violence! I will repeat this—there was NEVER any physical violence. But his actions, his reactions, his physical presence, his WORDS— they were and still are death!

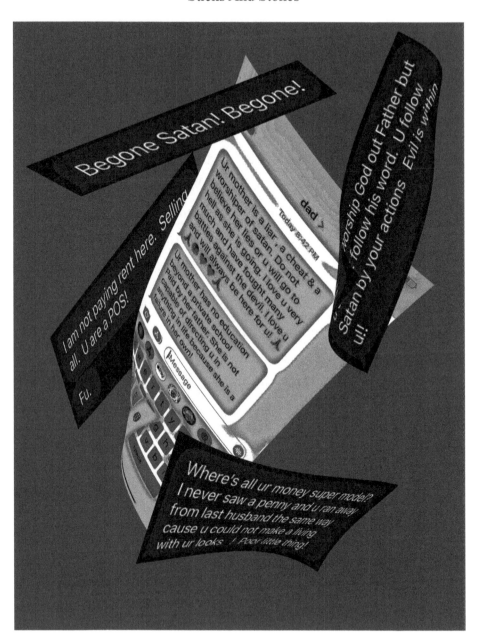

January 2022

Super Model? Even Mari called it a hobby for u!

I am not paying rent here. Selling all. U are a POS! @#$%!

Where's all ur money super model? I never saw a penny and u ran away from last husband the same way cause u could not make a living with your looks! Poor little thing!

I did not create any of your weakness. I even brought u all of your things here after you ran away from Ketchikan.

U say u worship God our Father but u do not follow his word. U follow Satan by your actions. Evil is within you!

Begone Satan! Begone!

As I am writing this, I am finally finalizing my divorce to this person.

When the children and I fled Alaska, they were still minors. Because of Ronald's unhinged response to our leaving—never once looking in the mirror and taking accountability for any of what transpired—we were awarded a four-year restraining order. The actions for divorce after that were long and drawn out. He was far from cooperative. After fifteen long months, I settled for a legal separation. That was awarded October 31, 2019.

It is April 19, 2022, and Ronald is being served the divorce papers.

Between the time of the legal separation and today, Ronald did come back into our lives. We dropped the restraining order, as I was blindly hopeful that we could work out what was broken in our marriage.

Why throw nineteen years away? There must be some healthy foundation left? Something to repair and possibly make better or even stronger.

That was my optimism and faith talking.

How could I be soooooo STUPID! Yes, you read it right. The children and I fled in the middle of the night. We were assisted by the Ketchikan Safe House and the Ketchikan Police. We were awarded a four-year restraining order. We had love and support from family and friends. We were under professional counseling. And then, when the legal separation was finalized, Ron showed up at our door in Michigan.

There were so many things I could have done. So many sane options, but NO! What does this woman do? I felt sorry for him and invited him BACK into our lives!

He's right, I must be insane! To be treated so horribly for so many years, for that oozing, nasty garbage to reveal itself on paper and in threats during the separation, and I still felt sorry for him? I must be addicted to abuse.

When Ronald appeared at our door, he looked pathetic. The once ruggedly handsome man looked old, broken, and on the verge of what you would imagine a homeless person to look like.

"I can't do this on my own, Jess." He pleaded with me. "You and the kids are my only friends."

My heart was racing. I was nervous, I was saddened, and I was concerned for his well-being.

Ronald arrived at the beginning of November. We were living in Traverse City, Michigan. Grand Traverse County in the winter on a warm day is twenty degrees, and that year we had the privilege to experience the polar vortex—ten days of temps -30 degrees or colder!

"Ron," I said with compassion, "you can't stay here, but I spoke with the manager, and she has another apartment available. See if you can rent it month to month until we can figure THIS out."

Ronald did rent a unit a block from us. We did not tell the kids right away. I wasn't sure how they would even react.

Our legal separation in the state of Alaska was finalized on October 31, 2019. On November 02, 2019, Ronald was on the ferry en route to finding his family. In tow, he had a car hauler with many family belongings, as well as our 1967 Shelby Mustang. The plan of action was to sell the house in Alaska and bring the Mustang to auction in West Palm Beach, Florida.

I needed a future and working for eleven dollars an hour at David's Bridal wasn't going to cut it. I was starting over at fifty-four years old.

"What am I going to do?" Those words haunted me every moment of every day. I could only accept financial help from my family for so long. I had to get my act together. Maybe Ron's coming here wasn't such a bad idea.

Maybe we could move forward. Sell the house, sell the car (historic race car) and start fresh as a family?

My therapist firmly advised against it, and when I went to the courts to have the restraining order dropped, the counselor asked me to take some time to think about it carefully. She had too many times seen women in my situation run back into that familiar space only for the situation to not heal but to get worse.

Did I listen? Of course not!

I am soooooo stupid!

Ronald did what Ronald does best. He put on that air of the caring, supportive, protective husband and father. I thought I could let my guard down and breathe again.

Yes, we can do this. I was convincing myself that anything is possible with God, and just maybe we were supposed to get back together.

As a family, we moved to Florida from the frigid temps of Michigan in January 2020. I will not pretend that everything was okay. In fact, the red flags started popping back up almost immediately. When there was any tension whatsoever, Ron would always throw in my face— "I never left you! You are the one who disappeared in the middle of the night. You should be grateful I am even here to take care of you."

Those words just made my stomach turn. I wasn't afraid this time; in fact, God was helping me find my courage. Instead of staying silent and cowering away, I would calmly respond to him with one question.

"Ron, have you ever once asked yourself what went so wrong that the kids and I had to leave the way we did?"

His response would be a stormy reaction—throwing accusations at me and denying he ever did anything wrong—only that he was always the victim.

"The victim—always the victim." I shrugged my shoulders.

It's not that I didn't care; it is just that I found my strength. The scales that had for so many years blinded me were gone. My perspective was new. I was watching a seventy-year-old man throwing a temper tantrum like a five-year-old.

Ronald was using the same old tactics to try to control the kids and me—to keep us playing by his rules. The only thing is, I was different. I was finding the Jessica that had disappeared so many years ago, and I no longer played by his rules.

This, of course, infuriated him. He could hold his tongue during the day and out in public; however, during the evening hours, when the family usually winds down and enjoys one another's company—that is when the insults would start. The condescending, vulgar, toxic words would be directed at me—more like thrust into me, like a dagger.

The new me would not react. I would simply take my glass of wine and remove myself from the room. I am human, so it's not that I no longer had emotion. My stomach would be in knots, but this time that wall of protection, that shield, would go up and keep me calm on the exterior. He hated that he could not get to me. Little did he know how terrified and broken I still was on the inside. Dare I let him get a glimpse of this, and he would have the upper hand again.

I am certain many of my readers are asking, "WHY? Why did you stay for so long? Why did you ever let him back in?"

Those are really good questions, and I wish I had a simple answer.

I guess it is because I was conditioned, and it was familiar. Familiarity can be a comfort zone.

It's a pattern. It's familiar, and something familiar can be comforting even if it's not healthy. I needed to feel that semblance of comfort again.

If my kids were happy, I would keep the door closed.

If I had a fabulous career, I would keep the door closed.

If...

Sadly, our fifteen months in Michigan seemed just as trying as when we were back in Ketchikan. Many circumstances were healthier, but the comfort of my own beautiful home was not there. The stability of my husband's income was not there. And to make matters worse, my children were still struggling, and the depression seemed to get worse.

My decisions, my actions, will determine their future!

Not to make excuses, but please remember, the first seven years of my marriage to this man were healthy. We built a foundation together. We worked together, had two beautiful children, and bought a home together.

Ronald has, or had, some admirable qualities and is liked by many. It's just, his personality started to divide. When in public, he was one way, and behind closed doors another. When it was all about Captain Ron, his accomplishments, and dreams, all was fine. When the attention turned towards me or the kids, it was his way or no way.

In these last two years, the time we did get back together, the smartest thing I ever did, was that I kept the legal separation in force and kept our finances separate.

Yes, we were living under the same roof, but as he fell back into the monster we ran away from, I prayed for strength. Strength to get through each day with a bit of sanity until either I could financially afford to move the kids and me out or I could at least get the kids off to college.

God blessed me and met me in the middle!

I was able to pick up a part-time job at a beautiful Christian Boutique. The time away from Ronald was incredibly healing. I was busy working with folks who appreciated my time and my abilities. Even if the hours at the shop were long, I felt renewed.

You know things aren't healthy at home when you dread leaving work to go back home.

It is the heart that makes a home, not the house.

Our rental house in Saint Augustine was beautiful. It was in a quaint, beachy neighborhood and directly across the street from the ocean. If just the kids and I lived there, it would have been a dream. Instead, Ronald brought with him his tormented soul and he made the environment toxic. Nothing I did was right. Nothing I did was good enough. All my decisions, according to my roommate (yes, I will call him this), were poor, insane, invalid or all of the above.

Our son was accepted to college. The campus was finally open after the long COVID-19 shutdown. Noah, who is on the autism spectrum, wanted to move out and go to school. His father thought it would be a waste of money!

Noah was falling back into anxiety attacks and depression.

"Baby," I said to my son, "I will figure out a way for you to go. You did the hard part and got accepted."

And I did. I turned over every stone. I investigated every possible grant, scholarship, and loan program out there. I, YES, I, without the assistance of Noah's father, was able to secure our son's college future and get him his own apartment. And to make things even sweeter, our daughter, Sophie, offered to be her big brother's roommate.

With Noah's autism, we knew he would need help with his daily routine and were a bit concerned about a random roommate, really a stranger, being part of Noah's introduction into college life. Sophia was entering her senior year in high school. She had a job and had just purchased her first car. (That is another story we could clearly vent about).

"Mom, I'll be Noah's roommate," she insisted. "It makes the most sense. I know all his quirks and I will be there for him!"

"But what about school and your job?" I asked as almost an automatic response but knew too well where this was going and honestly, I couldn't be more relieved.

"I'm already taking classes online; I'll just transfer over to full time online. And work? I promise I'll pick up a job as soon as we get settled in the apartment." She pleaded. "I can't live here anymore with him." Sophe was referring to her father. "He is negative about EVERYTHING!"

"I get it, baby," I muttered to myself.

"Okay, then," I exclaimed.

"Okay! REALLY?" she was beyond excited.

"You know this won't go over well with your dad? But then again, nothing ever does." I took a very deep breath, my stomach knotting up again.

I was going to make this happen for the kids, regardless of Ron's insane reasoning. Our children need a future, and he wants to hold them hostage! I knew I was going to have to face another demon and step into this battle.

God, please get me through this unscathed!

April 16, 2022

Ur mother is a liar, a cheat & a worshiper of Satan. Do not believe her lies or u will go to hell as she is going. I love u very much and have fought many battles against the devil. I love u and will always be here for u! (Praying hands emoji, praying hands emoji, kissing face emoji, heart emoji, heart emoji, praying hands emoji)

Ur mother has no education beyond a private school paid by her father. She is not

capable of directing u in anything in life
because she is a failure in her own!

ALL ROADS LEAD HOME

As the saying goes, home is where the heart is.

We travel so many roads in this life. Some are dusty, kicked up dirt roads where we meander for years. Others are sleek and fast—lightning speed. But whatever road we happen to be on at the moment, I believe it is not by coincidence. God has purposely placed us on a path to lead us home. As we wander through life, our will and God's ultimate plan for us intertwine.

I mention our will and God's plan, because most of the time, we are not aligned with God's purpose for our lives. We are driven by the physical wants and needs of this life, with a certain amount of satisfaction as a reward. What we are missing is that our aim is inferior to that which God has created for us. The good news is, He puts up roadblocks, detours, and other obstacles to reroute us back to His glorious path.

So how does another woman fit into this equation? The

other woman. Just the thought of it makes my stomach queasy—all these years and you think you know someone! I will start by saying I never had trust issues. My marriage wasn't perfect; however, trusting my husband to be faithful wasn't a concern that ever crossed my mind. Boy, was I naïve? It was as if their relationship had started off in the shadows, and as I kept pushing down my "gut" feelings and denying anything was going on between them, they became bolder, and their flirtatious behavior was flaunted right in front of my eyes. Sadly, I became numb to the extramarital affair, dismissing it as though I were being paranoid and hormonal.

Dawn was my friend. We met at one of those "Pampered Chef" type parties, only instead, this one was for skin care. Dawn is about five years younger than me. We share similar backgrounds. Both of us were fashion models. She was discovered by Jonny Casablanca and worked in LA with Elite while I was the East Coast gal—New York City with Eileen Ford. Dawn was—beautiful. Auburn hair, green eyes, perfect complexion with the dusting of freckles and to wrap this package of perfection up, she has a very feisty personality. Although our temperaments are opposite ends of the spectrum, we connected as friends.

I was actually excited to introduce my new friend to Ronald. Dawn held qualities that I had yet to achieve and having similar backgrounds as models, bolstered who I was as a person.

Let me explain. Although Captain Ron bragged to others that I was a fashion model when we first met, I was not a seafaring type of gal, nor was I a survivalist knowing or even wanting to know how to live off the land—hunt, fish, and the like. I was eager and capable for the adventure, but my skill set was on a learning curve.

As our marriage got on in years, Ronald found ways to dismiss and degrade the career that I had prior. He would put it down as meaningless, empty, and selfish. He wouldn't blurt these insults out—rather, he would find a way to incorporate them into a conversation twisting the facts in some weird way, to make it sound like he had a valid point.I truly enjoyed my career as a fashion model. It was a blessing and a dream come true. Because of my passion for my earlier career, I did have the sense to defend my experience in the fashion industry. However, his barrage of insults would not stop after one occasion—this went on for years. It got to the point that I wouldn't even react to his opinion rather, I simply dismissed Ronald's negative commentary. Conversations in our home were not the traditional definition of a conversation. You know, when two or more people talk, engaging in a thought process and exchanging ideas or various points of view? Ronald would talk...no...more like lecture us. If we dared to introduce an opinion other than his, it would quickly get dismissed, put down or, mysteriously, not get heard at all. He was right, and that was that.

Fast forward to Dawn. Not only did she have a modeling career, but Dawn was also a very skilled hunter and fisherwoman. She held attributes that I knew would impress my husband. So why would I want to introduce someone like this to Ron? Simple. As I mentioned earlier, I never had trust issues or low self-esteem. My intention was to introduce a friend who had a similar background to mine (defending the modeling career) and was also very skilled at what Ronald thought was worthy.

Dawn and I weren't best friends, yet we did get together quite frequently. Where do I even begin? Okay, Vicki. Victoria is Dawn's 17-year-old daughter. Victoria is exquisitely beautiful—Nastassja Kinski kind of beautiful. With me being a photographer and Dawn and I both having been models, we teamed up to develop a portfolio for Vicki. This project lasted for the better part of a year. From simple beauty sessions, to full on fashion/editorial spreads—we spent a good amount of time together.

To help compensate me for my time working on Vicki's portfolio, several times a year (February/ March in particular) Dawn would hire my Captain Ron to run one of the lodge catamarans for the various fisheries. During herring season, before the fishery would open—Ketchikan Sac Roe Herring Fishery—Ron and Dawn would take the corporate executives out to run samples on the herring eggs, also known as roe. These jobs could last days, if not weeks, at a time with hours running from 6:00 a.m. to as late as 2:00 a.m.

Again, I did not have trust issues. I had my hands full with the kids, their activities, my photography and, honestly, this opportunity—Ronald working with Dawn—was some extra household income that I was grateful for.

Having Dawn and her daughter over to the house became fairly regular. From dropping by to see if Ronnie could help Dawn fix something that went wrong with a rifle to, "Hey Jess, just caught some snapper and I know how to make a mean ceviche, what time should we come by?" kinda relationship. It was easy, effortless and…comfortable. Almost like we had known one another for years.

Red flag—over the years, it was becoming too comfortable. Dawn was at the house too often.

"Hey Jess, look who dropped by," Ron would eagerly announce, even though Dawn was standing right in front of me.

"Hi," I would respond, taking groceries out of the car, unloading kids or something.

"Everything okay? How are things with Vicki?" I would ask.

"Yeah, everything's fine. Just driving by and saw your hubby out working on the boat. Thought he could use some help," she quickly responded.

"Yes, babe," he would shout down from the boat in a giddy kind of tone. "You weren't home, and I needed an extra pair of hands."

Another red flag. Ronald never called me "babe" unless he was up to something.

Or when I came home one day, and Dawn and Ronald were in the garage together. I had pulled up in the driveway and the garage door was open. My husband was showing her how to disassemble and reassemble a firearm. I just stood there watching them from the driveway. Their proximity to one another and body language was so much more than just two "friends." It truly was a slap in my face. When I approached and let them know that I was home, they didn't even acknowledge me.

"Oh, when did you get back? Didn't even see you there." my husband simply remarked with a flat tone to his voice.

Of course, he didn't see me; he was so wrapped up in her and she in him. Their relationship was right in front of me, on display, and I just took it.

What had happened to me? Who had I become?

God gives us "gut" feelings for a reason. Why was I continually pushing them away?

And then the icing on the cake—the little white Mercedes. This is a good one—a good one to highlight how stupid I was.

Ronald's brother, Cameron, was visiting for a few weeks. It happened to be in August and my birthday is in August. For my readers to understand, in all the years Ronald and I were together, he never surprised me with flowers or really a gift of any kind. Actually, I take that back. On our first date, he bought me a bouquet of red roses, probably to impress me and get beyond first base. Other gifts over the years would be more for himself than for me—an AR-15, for instance, or how about that 45 mm I always wanted? Yeah, right?

On this particular birthday, when Cam was visiting, Ronald came home with a gorgeous bouquet of flowers and a bottle of champagne. Being the good, considerate wife that I am, of course, I thanked him. I also thanked Cameron for reminding him.

"Oh, Ronnie didn't forget your birthday, Jess. I just had to remind him that he was not going home empty-handed," Cam responded in a joking manner.

"Well, thank you both for remembering me."

It was during this visit that we saw a little white Mercedes convertible for sale. Ketchikan is a very small and remote town in the southeast region of Alaska. The Coast

Guard is a huge part of our community. Every three years, the CG families are rotated, so we not only have to say "goodbye" to friends, but we also gain new faces. During these rotations, many sell their belongings to make the move easier. Long story short, a CG officer was selling his little white Mercedes for a good price.

"Ronnie!" Cameron exclaimed. "You should buy that little convertible for Jessie. She would look so sweet driving it around."

"Oh, honey!" reaching over and squeezing my hubby's shoulders, "that would be so much fun."

I always left purchases like this up to Ron, but somehow, I got excited. Like this idea was possible and to my surprise, Ronald seemed to be onboard! Over the next couple of days, we made the phone calls, test drove this little gem and….as I was thinking we were actually going to move forward and make the purchase, Ronald convinced me that it would not be a good investment.

I'm not going to lie. I was disappointed. Maybe he was right. It was only a car, after all. Nevertheless, my heart sank.

Punch in the gut. Three days later. Three days after Ronald convinced me that buying that little white Mercedes convertible for me was not a good investment. Only three days. Can you guess? And who comes zipping by and pulls up in our driveway in her new little white Mercedes convertible?

Coincidence? Could be, but my gut was screaming, and tears swelled up in my eyes. Do I have physical evidence that he bought this little gem for his lover? No, I do not. What I do know is that these two were blatantly having an affair and now taunting me. I can only imagine what they were saying about me behind my back.

And this was not the first fling he'd had. There was another, although brief, when I was expecting our son. I chalked those feelings up to hormonal paranoias; however, looking back and better understanding the signs of one engaging in an affair—well, my instincts were correct.

Dawn and Ronald continued in their "union." It was becoming more apparent that this behavior was acceptable to my husband because he did not regard me as his wife, but rather an appendage —a part of him. It was as if the "we" made "him" whole, and Dawn was his to have a relationship with.

Yes, it is extremely difficult to relive and write this all down. I still cry years later. What I do know is that I tried.

I tried to be a good wife. I tried to be a real friend. I tried to be his advocate. In the process, I lost myself. I crumbled and went through a very dark and tormented time, struggling between what was happening and what I knew life should be. On the outside, I managed to keep it all together, but my kids knew, my family knew.

"Jessie, you need to hire an attorney and get a divorce. He will never change; he will only drag you and the kids down—it's a sinking ship." Those words from my sister, Natalie, kept repeating in my brain.

"Jessie, if you can't do this for yourself, for God's sake, do it for the kids. How will they see you when any dreams they had evaporated because their mom was too weak to protect them?" These were harsh but concerned words from my sister, Grace.

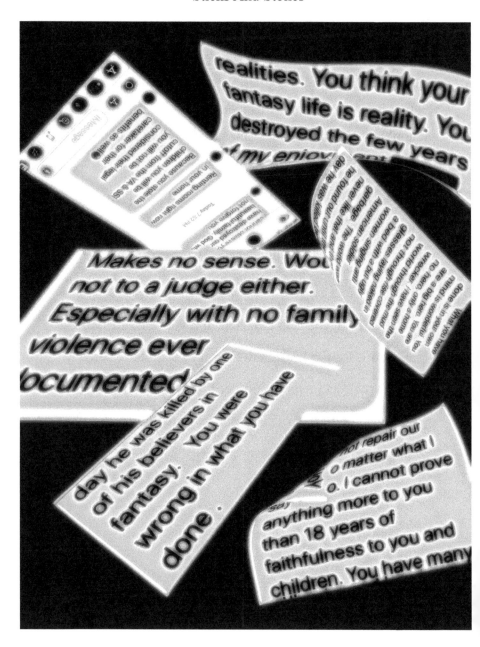

Text from Ronald after we left:

You think your fantasy life is reality. You have destroyed the few years of my enjoyment. What you have done is in your own mind and is wonderful. You are a big hero. You are no hero, only a home wrecker. I have seen the world through the mud not through rose covered glasses laying naked in bed with a butt ugly woman singing anti American solder garbage. The world was never like that until I found out the day, I was killed by one of my believers in fantasy. You were wrong in what you have done. I cannot believe you have destroyed our beautiful family. I cannot prove anything more to you than 18 years of faithfulness to you and the children. Makes no sense, especially with no family violence ever documented. God will not forgive you.

Actions speak louder than words; yet words have a cutting edge—they can be that fatal blow. Wow! The years have taken their toll, but God kept a spark alive and breathed a new life into me.

The other woman was not a roadblock or even a detour. The other woman was a ditch that I had to climb out of to see a new perspective. I had to peel away the denial. I had to acknowledge that I had worth and did not deserve the way I was being treated. I had to see that the dreams I have carried with me were placed on my heart by God for a reason. These dreams are real and not some fantasy. This ditch that I fell into carried me to a stronger place.

A dear friend of mine would often say to me, "Be careful what you wish for."

My response?

"Why did you say to me, 'Be careful what you wish for?' In my book, a wish is the same as a dream. A dream is placed in your heart by God. Never be afraid to dream—life is far too short. And dreams do come true! Just sayin'

Remember, God's plan is superior to anything we could ever dream up for ourselves.

A Measure of ...

"Sophia!" I screamed. "Lock the doors!"

"Noah, you have to calm down!" My heart was racing as my son was having a severe anxiety attack and trying to jump out of the car.

"NOAH! Please, baby, take a deep breath." I was screaming at this point to try to snap him out of the suicidal place he was in.

"Sophie, the nearest hospital—put it in the GPS" I was trying desperately to think through this very dark moment. My 14-year-old was rushing to help me.

It was three days after my brother's funeral. The children and I had flown out to California from Michigan when Charlie was being intubated. The prognosis was not good; however, half-full is a lot better than half empty and knowing my brother's thirst for life—miracles do happen!

"The machines will allow his body to rest and heal." his doctors assured us. "Your brother has so much scar tissue on his lungs, the energy it takes for him to breathe is taking away from any healing process that can move him forward…" or something like that. The medical terms being thrown around were just a jumble of words to me. I just wanted my brother to rest, to heal, and to come back to us.

Grace had arrived the day before and went straight to the hospital. I scrambled and booked one-way tickets from Traverse City, Michigan to San Francisco, California for the kids and myself, and we joined my sister by Charlie's side the next day.

"Hey," I said, hugging my sister in the hall, "how is he doing? Where is Andrea?"

"Andrea is at home. I told her to go and get some rest." Grace gave me a hug. "Just want you to be prepared before you go in. He is hooked up on life support," she said in a somber tone, holding back tears.

"I know, but it will be okay," I reassured her. "This will give his body a chance to rest." I was numb, but my heart was convincing me it was going to be all right, and we had to be optimistic for Charlie!

When I walked into the hospital room, he looked so

beautiful, so peaceful. Aside from all the machinery, he had good color, and his vitals were encouragingly healthy. That was a good day. Grace, Charlie's friend Mark, and I sat with Charlie all day. Although the audible exchange in conversation was only between those visiting and the nursing staff, I know for a fact that Charlie chimed in on several occasions.

"Gross," Mark's expression said it all as I was rubbing Charlie's very dirty feet. Not dirty per se, but all the dead skin that accumulates when you don't scrub regularly.

"What? He loves his feet rubbed—dirty or not." I simply smiled back. "Maybe if I find a ticklish spot, he'll sit up and yell at me to stop."

"Or you are just torturing him," Grace remarked.

"Oh, no!" I jumped back. "I'm sorry Charlie."

The hours got on. Mark left for the evening and Grace insisted that I go back to the hotel with the kids. She would spend the evening with Charlie in the hospital room. She promised we could switch posts the next day.

"Promise? This will be the third night you have slept on that cot," I said.

"I promise." She coaxed me towards the door. "Hey sis, I love you!"

"Luv you, too."

"Coffee—when you come in the morning, can you bring Starbucks?"

"Absolutely!"

We didn't have a plan. Only that we were going to stay as long as Andrea needed us and take one day at a time.

One day at a time. If only I could string together another twenty years of "one day at a time."

I'm going to stop right here and tell my readers—NO, I'm going to insist—DO NOT TAKE ANYTHING FOR GRANTED! Hug those you love and tell them over and over again how much you love them.

We never got that reassurance of "one day at a time."

"Jessie," I answered my phone at 5:40 a.m. and only hearing my sister gasping for breath. "It's… It's not…"

Grace couldn't even finish her sentence. I woke the kids, and we rushed to the hospital.

A Measure Of . . .

All I can remember is running as fast as I could. I rushed through the ICU doors and straight into Charlie's room. Grace was standing in the corner, looking out the window with tears streaming down her cheeks. My brother was no longer with us. He was lying there, perfectly cleaned up. His body was at rest. And I just lost it!

"He can't be—" I started screaming at God. "Please, Lord, please, make him one of your miracles! Wake my brother up—PLEASE!" I continued sobbing.

Time stood still. We were all numb and in disbelief. Andrea was sitting outside his room. She couldn't bear seeing her husband, her true love, gone. They really were a match made in heaven.

As the hands of the clock continued to move us into the day, accepting the fact that God had taken my brother home was becoming a harsh reality. Family and friends had joined us at the hospital for support, and now and in the days to come, we had to plan a funeral.

Brother -

The definition of BROTHER according to the Webster Dictionary is:

Sticks And Stones

A male who has the same parents as another or one parent in common with another
One related to another by common ties or
interests

A fellow member – used as a title for min-
isters in some evangelical denominations
One who shares with another a common
national or racial origin especially: soul
brother[2]

Charlie embodies every essence of the word.
My brother IS larger than life. He knows how to
not only test the waters, but dive into the deep end
and figure it out along the way. His laughter, his
wit, his compassion, his thirst for adventure, his
LOVE for life...

Charlie IS!

I am purposely using the present tense as Charlie IS still with us. Each and every one he has touched holds and cherishes a part of him.

You don't have to be in the same room with Charlie to enjoy his presence…just knowing that he is out there in the world some place stirring up trouble is comfort enough.

I will always hear his voice saying, "Hey Sis…" and knowing that I am usually the last to know "what's up." Well, I'll take pride that although I might be the last, I was never the least in his book!

There is nothing to sum up, because Charlie IS still with us.

To my amazing baby brother—CHEERS!

Charlie passed on October 4, 2018.

"Fitting," my sister said.

"What?" I was confused at what she was referring to.

"Do you know what day it is? October 4—you know, 10-4, over and out."

I chuckled and looked up. "Thanks brother, you always knew how to get the last word in."

I don't know if it is befitting to call a funeral beautiful, but in all essence of the word, this one was. There was so much love and light. We buried my brother along the Pacific Coast, where he could smell the salt in the air, hear the crashing of the waves, and swim the depths of the ocean he so often fished. Charlie was home!

Now it was time for me to figure out a way for my kids and me to get back home to Michigan. I was running on empty, and my financial situation was near scraping the bottom of the barrel. I probably could have reached out to friends and family, but for some reason, my pride was determined to be creative and do this on my own. I could not afford three airline tickets, but how about a rental car?

"Kids, up for a road trip?" I asked them enthusiastically, trying to cover up a desperate plea.

"Sure?" they both answered questionably.

"Money is slightly tight, so I was thinking we could

take this time and drive back. Three to five days, max. Maybe stop and visit Jean and Emma in Arizona on the way back?"

"Okay." Sophie was on board.

"Noah, sweetie, what do you think?"

"What about school? I've already missed a week." He was becoming uncomfortable about falling behind, and a routine for Noah was incredibly important.

"I've already spoken with your counselor, and she promised me you won't skip a beat. Because of everything we are going through, she can have a few assignments waived." Reassuring my son that this would be okay. "So, are you onboard?"

"Okay, guess so," he shrugged his shoulders.

"Thanks, baby," I said, giving them both a huge squeeze. "Memories in the making—here we come!"

The kids and I hit the road the day after the funeral. Our first stop was back at my sister Natalie's house to see if we could convince my mom to join us on this adventure. Mom had been residing with my elder sister for the last year in the sweet village of Cambria, California. I was comforted to know that she was not alone. Nat and I were both thinking that a road trip might be a good distraction for our mom and, in turn, some emotional support for me. When we arrived, Mom was, understandably, not feeling well, let alone in a place to travel. Not wanting to delay the inevitable—Michigan, here we come!

The kids and I took the southern route as our Ketchikan friends, Jean and Emma, had moved to Scottsdale, Arizona during our whole ordeal. They insisted that we come by and stay at least a night or two with them. It would be wonderful to see some familiar faces to break up the trip.

When you think things are finally falling into a place—at least a solid ground kinda place—then the rug is pulled out yet again!

"God, I don't know if I can take anymore!" I was focused, but numb. I was just a shell of myself, trying desperately to hold it together.

We had made it to Arizona without incident. We were only an hour away from our friend's home. What happened?

"Noah, baby—PLEASE CALM DOWN!" I was screaming at the top of my lungs, desperate to snap him out of this panic attack.

I was driving on the freeway at eighty mph when Noah

had a meltdown. I hadn't noticed, but his anxiety had built up to a place that he couldn't handle it, or life, anymore. My 16-year-old son tried to jump out of the SUV. Thank goodness the vehicle we rented locked automatically when in gear and it had backdoor baby locks.

"What do I do? What do I do?" I kept muttering to myself.

"Hospital! Sophia, baby, find me the nearest hospital."

God is amazing. Two exits from where Noah's initial outburst happened, there was a Mayo Clinic.

"Ma'am, what's going on?" the emergency room attendant asked.

"My son has autism, and he is having a severe anxiety attack. He tried to jump out of a moving car!" I blurted out, trying to stay somewhat composed and not cry.

"It will be okay. We'll take him back while I have you fill out some paperwork," the attendant said in a consoling manner.

"We're from out of state. We are headed back to Michigan from California."

"Do you have any friends or family here?" The questions continued.

"Yes, we are planning to stay with friends in Scottsdale. Oh shoot, Sophie, baby, can you text Jean?"

I realized I needed to call Jean to let her know what was going on. God bless her. She dropped whatever she was doing and came straight to the hospital.

"OMG, girl, it's sooooo good to see you!" I could hear her animated voice as she came running through the emergency entrance doors. Needless to say, major hugs from my friend were more than welcome.

"Are you okay? How's Noah? Hey, Sophie, sweetie, why don't you and I surprise Em at school? You come with me and let your mom spend some time with your brother and the doctors." Jean always had a hand on the pulse of things.

"Thank you so much—for everything! Love you," I said, giving my friend another big squeeze.

"Love you back."

The girls took off, and I sat with Noah in the emergency exam room. The doctors had given him some medication to calm his nerves and help him sleep.

"Ms. Millard, let's wait and see how your son is feeling when he wakes up. That will give us a better idea whether we should admit him for observation overnight or if he can leave with you."

Acknowledging, I nodded my head.

Noah was out cold. He slept for about three hours. I'm certain I nodded off a few times myself. We were exhausted. I mean, exhausted to the core. Only two months prior, we fled a very toxic domestic environment, leaving behind a life we had become accustomed to; were in the process of trying to grasp everything, including the fact that we were just awarded a four-year restraining order against my husband. And then my brother died. No wonder my son had an anxiety attack. I don't blame him. Everyone, typical or not, has a boiling point. My baby just happened to hit his limit on our road trip.

"Hey, Noah!" Emma came bounding in with her arms filled with stuff. She, Sophie, and Jean stopped by the gift store and bought Noah a huge stuffed teddy bear, balloons, a get-well card, and chocolates, which, by the way, I commandeered.

"How are you feeling, buddy?" she continued.

"Embarrassed." He responded sheepishly, wanting to hide under the blanket.

"Nonsense, we all have our [expletive]—oops, I mean stuff. Sorry mom." Em quickly apologizing for her choice of words.

"Are you staying, or can we have a pizza party tonight?" she continued.

At that time, the doctor came in.

"So how is my patient feeling? You look a lot better." The physician was looking over Noah's chart and checking his vitals once again. "Think you are up for hanging out with your friends? Much better company than us old folks here." Doc slipped in a bit of humor to lighten the mood.

"Sure, I guess," Noah responded.

We were discharged from the hospital around 4:30 p.m. and headed over to Jean's house, which was about forty minutes away. When we arrived, I was so ready to collapse on the sofa with a glass of wine in hand. I was "so" ready; however, the evening had one more card to play out.

My son's anxiety had not dissipated completely; in fact, it had transformed into anger and frustration. When I walked into the master bedroom to bring Noah supper, he not only grabbed the tray from me and threw it, but he also lunged at me, grabbing me by the throat. This behavior had

NEVER happened before.

"911!" I screamed, as I was pushing myself away and trying to hold Noah's arms down, away from my neck.

"Someone call 911!"

Jean came rushing in and grabbed Noah from behind. Between the two of us, we were able to get him flat on the ground on his stomach. Just for reference, my son is 6'1" with a slight build; however, his strength was magnified during this episode.

The paramedics arrived and back to the hospital we went. This time, they admitted my son for further observation.

Noah was discharged early afternoon the following day with the recommendation that we fly back to Michigan. The medical team recognized that routine was a comfort zone and Noah needed some semblance of routine to calm his nerves. Medication was also prescribed to ease the balance of our trip. Honestly, I could have used something to calm my nerves as well.

Heading back to a place that is not quite your home seems strange. Michigan wasn't meant to be my home, and I knew that deep down. It was my sister's home. I was in a holding pattern and Traverse City—the love and support from my family, the community, and new friends— was only going to be temporary. It offered a sound base while things fell into place.

Text Message from Cameron Millard (Ronald's Brother):

> You have made an enemy that will never forget or forgive you for what you are doing to my brother. You are a lying, manipulating, downright EVIL woman who has ruined a man that loved you. May you rot in Hell!
> How IS Michigan anyway? Liar!

Text messages from Ronald:

> Do you really believe you are following God's Word or the teachings of JESUS!
> I would like to buy air tickets for the kids to go to Charlie's funeral. I would like permission to go to the funeral too. He was part of my family for 19 years.

Post from Ronald on my Facebook page –

Charles "Charlie" passed from this earth today. Charlie was a great catcher of hearts and fish. Pray his soul enters the Kingdom of Heaven and for the healing of the hearts of those that love him. In Jesus name, Amen!

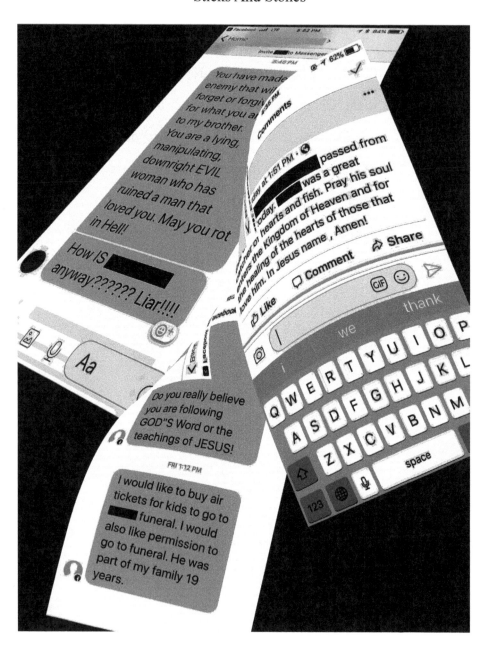

Georgia on My Mind

My head was on the pillow. Lying in bed, I stared up at the ceiling as thoughts drifted in and out of my mind. Four years of commotion, four years of struggle, four years of determination, and a newfound faith were under my belt.

It was as if my life was a pearl necklace that broke. Precious jewels that scattered all over the floor. I was finding and picking up each—one at a time. Many were right in front of me, while others had rolled into dark corners, or even found their way down crevices in the floorboards. Individual gems—love, loss, hope, fear, faith, courage, trust, tolerance, and a host of others.

I was battle weary and scarred, but I hadn't come this far to give up. If anything, I had gained a new perspective, one that would hopefully be a firm foundation for a healthier future. Trust would be one of my biggest hurdles moving forward, but at least I was willing to recognize that.

"Hello?" My 86-year-old aunt answered the phone.

"Auntie Marianthe, it's Jessie." I had called her from the car. "There is a surprise that should have been delivered; can you go to your front door?"

"A surprise for me?" she inquired.

"Yes," I said, trying to contain myself.

It was November 07, 2021. Auntie Mari's health was not good. I had received a phone call from my other aunt the evening before—10:00 p.m., to be exact. Auntie Beverly was very concerned about her sister and asked if there was any way I could make the trip from Saint Augustine, Florida to Savannah, Georgia, in the next couple of days.

"Absolutely," I said without hesitation. "I can leave first thing in the morning. It's only about a three-hour drive."

"Oh, Jessie, I can't thank you enough. You don't know how much this means to me!" I could hear the relief in Bev's voice. "Do me one more favor? Don't tell Mari you are coming. She will insist that she is fine. She is stubborn that way."

"Don't you worry…mum's the word. I just don't want to give her a heart attack when I show up at the door," I added, trying to lighten the concern.

My Aunt Marianthe was a retired physician. She was eighty-six years young, with a mind as sharp as a tack. It was her heart that was compromising her health. Her condition was such that it was only time.

Ronald was listening in as I was speaking with my Aunt Bev. When I hung up, he asked when I planned to go and insisted on joining me. I was not surprised. In fact, it was reassuring that he wanted to come. I do know that my aunt liked Ron. She had always enjoyed his immense knowledge of history and the stories he would share. I would much rather have him as a friend than a foe, especially during this time.

Ronald came back into our lives after a fifteen-month separation. Although we were legally separated, we decided to try and mend our differences and salvage the marriage. It had been almost two years now, and we were treading on very thin ice. Ronald would not accept accountability for anything that had gone wrong in the past. In his mind, he was, and would always be, the victim. I was the one to blame. I was the one who destroyed the family—threw everything away because of a selfish whim.

Nineteen years together, fifteen months apart, and now two years under the same roof—we were desperately trying to take hold of any healthy parts of our marriage, focusing on what brought us together and working on healing what was broken. The only problem was that the "healthy part" was a mere bread crumb. His disdain for me was tangible. Life behind closed doors was returning to what the children and I had fled. If I kept the focus on Ronald and Ronald's interests, the atmosphere was calm. As soon as the focus shifted, his tolerance vanished. We, rather, I was the targeted enemy out to destroy a version of life that he found satisfactory.

I will be the first to admit that I had changed. I found the Jessica that was lost years ago. I was willing to work with Ronald on our relationship; however, this time, I was unwilling to cower and walk on eggshells. I had found my autonomy.

Unfortunately, or fortunately, Captain Ron no longer liked me, let alone use the word love. I actually believe he loathed me because he did not succeed in breaking me. He was nearly there. I was so close to becoming a shell of myself to accommodate his needs. Praise God for keeping that last spark alive!

"Oh my, Jessie! What are you doing here?" Auntie Mari's face was beaming when she saw me at the door.

"We came to visit with you for a few days, if that is, okay?" I said, as I was giving my aunt a hug.

"We?" she inquired, peering over towards the car.

"Yes. Ron came with me."

"I am so happy. Of course, please come in. But you know I was not expecting visitors so…" Auntie Mari was always so proud of preparing for her guests and being the wonderful hostess that comes naturally to her.

"I know. We came to see you, and we can fend for ourselves," I insisted.

"How long will you be staying?" she asked.

"As long as you can put up with us," I said jokingly.

Ronald and I ended up staying for about a week with my aunt. During this time frame, I was able to get a better grasp on the severity of her heart condition and update other family members. Moving forward, we knew that Auntie Mari's health was failing and that we would need to make accommodations for someone to check in or stay with her on a regular basis.

Another page in the book of life was being turned; however, we are not saying our goodbyes to Dr. Marian-the—not yet!

My aunt's failing health was a trigger for Ronald. He was more than willing to support me for one trip to Savannah, but how dare I volunteer to help and participate in my aunt's caregiving? This was unacceptable, nor would it be tolerated. According to Ronald, I was abandoning my position as a wife and a mother, even though our children were young adults living on their own. My place was to be attached to his side 24/7. I was to resume the job of propping up his ego, assisting him in his projects, and to be always at his disposal.

To add insult to injury, with money almost always being tight, I picked up a part-time position at a beautiful boutique in town. One would think that my husband would be happy, or at least supportive in my added efforts to not only take care of the home and the family, but to help bring in some additional income. No. In fact, he was angry. He was raging because he lost control.

I was a very faithful wife. I took my marriage seriously. Even when he abused the trust, I did not stoop to his level. As long as we lived under one roof, legally separated or not, I was going to respect the fact that we were trying.

December 30, 2021

"You are insane!" he said in a callous tone. "You would abandon your own children and spend New Year's with an aunt who chose to live alone her entire life?"

I just looked at Ron with a blank stare. He had been criticizing my family and my decision to help my aunt for the better part of a month. It was daily. It was a calculated onslaught in an attempt to unnerve me. Out of respect (possibly for myself), I would keep Ronald informed of tentative plans; however, I would not discuss in depth my aunt's caregiving needs. He was a master of manipulation, and he would twist this to fuel a fire—a fire that he hoped would consume any strength I had left.

It was 6:30 a.m. Ronald was standing by his bedroom door in his boxers, glaring at me as I was gathering my belongings. I had promised my aunt that we would ring in the New Year together. I only intended to be away for five days.

"You don't care. All about you. Nothing will change. You know everything. I am just an idiot that needs you." His attempts to demean me and make me feel less as a person failed.

As his insulting words and then texts continued to pour out, it finally hit. I took a deep breath, suitcase in hand, and headed out the door, never to return. I drove to Savannah and spent a wonderful week with my aunt. During this time, my kids and family were caught up on my status.

Ronald continued to text:

U are everything! I am nothing! U are brilliant! I am an idiot! Pass it on to our children momma!

Tell them I was not their dad! But Einstein like ur dad

U left me because I was too smart

To bad ur family didn't have money I could claim in marriage

Send it onto ur sis

I gave you everything I have and had before we met. What have u given me and our children other than childbirth which u asked me for and I was there for the last years until and even after u ran away for greener pastures.

Come on Einstein?

Waiting for brilliance!

Everything we have is yours because u gave birth to our children or because?

Waiting for ur intelligent response to questions u are capable to answer in court!

I am an idiot! U and ur sisters are brilliant!

I gave u everything in duress to try and give

our children all I had obtained in our legal

conjoining and Godly agreements before all

Christian requirements according to GOD.

I do not hate Ron. I don't think my heart has that capability or capacity. What I do hate is how he treated his family. His mental illness destroyed three families—ours being the third. The man I fell in love with was an act. He portrayed himself one way, and as the years matured, his true nature fell into play as he felt more at ease. His web of lies became a version of our reality. The more I questioned my husband, the tighter the noose became, and I began questioning myself. The children and I woke up in the middle of a nightmare; however, this nightmare was their entire existence.

I had a life before Ronald—that was the spark that kept me going. God kept reminding me through friendships, movies, music, and, most importantly, 'gut' feelings that I had to give my children a healthier life. The fight that I had to endure meant walking away from the comfort of a life that we built over two decades.

Ronald claims he gave me everything. The sad truth is, he stole years of happiness from us. The children and I walked away not once, but twice, leaving him with all the marital assets. In return, he threatened and insulted me.

Four years… or was it twenty-two?

I can't turn back the clock. Even if I could, I'm not sure that I would. I have been blessed with two amazing children, a family who truly cares, and friends who embrace and support me. I had to fall to my knees and "look up." God is the only One who can help me, or really any of us.

Is it part of His plan? Perhaps.

What I do know is that God is real! He is our Creator, and we are here for His glory.

He paved a way and navigated me through some very dark times. The waters I travel are still a bit choppy, but today… today my son is wrapping up his first year in college. My daughter graduated from high school and has landed herself a dream job. I am spending time with my beautiful aunt, who just happens to be my godmother. Though many days still bring tears, they also bring joy, more than I can remember. The shackles are off. I am free to come and go as I please, but most importantly, I am free to dream.

It was midnight. The Pennsylvania Polka by The Andrews Sisters was playing on a vintage record player…

"Jess," Auntie Mari called me into her room.

"Yes, ma'am," I responded with a smile.

"Dance the polka for me."

" Umm, the polka? I don't know how," I responded.

Up jumped all eighty pounds of this beautiful woman. Grabbing me by the hands, she showed me how to dance the polka. Her smile—so youthful, so vibrant, lit up my world!

On September 18, 2018, at 7:48 a.m. I sent an email to my estranged husband.

> I know you want to hear some elaborated
> story of why we left … the truth is quite
> simple. We left because you said we could.
> You said to me many times … "I'm not
> holding you back, there is the door. You can
> leave whenever you want." We did because
> we were tired of waiting on you. We did

because we were tired of all your excuses of why Ketchikan was the most beautiful and safest place on the planet. We did because we were tired of your drinking and how angry you were all the time. We did because …

There is no one else. Never has been. There is just a healthier and happier life out here.

You can either accept this or not.

Nothing fancy.

You can look in the mirror and either get some help or not.

You can drum up all the stories you want to or not.

OR

You can accept the fact that our marriage and life at home was broken … and instead of being angry and hateful towards me …

Change what went wrong or, at the very least, try.

You have a beautiful home. Enjoy it. You

have all the material things we worked so hard for. Enjoy them. I did not strip those from you.

And someday … possibly you will have a healthier relationship with your children.

Little wonders—life is a myriad of moments; good, bad and all the shades in-between. God is here to guide us, pick us up when we fall, and help us wipe off our skinned knees. Never stop dreaming—not until you take that last breath! The lyrics to this song seem to sum it up so beautifully:

"Little Wonders"

by Rob Thomas

Songwriters: Thomas Robert Kelly

Let it go

Let it roll right off your shoulder

Don't you know?

The hardest part is over

Let it in

Let your clarity define you

Georgia On My Mind

In the end

We will only just remember how it feels

Our lives are made

In these small hours

These little wonders

These twists and turns of fate

Time falls away

But these small hours

These small hours

Still remain

Let it slide

Let your troubles fall behind you

Let it shine

'Til you feel it all around you

And I don't mind

If it's me you need to turn to

We'll get by

It's the heart that really matters in the end

Our lives are made

In these small hours

These little wonders

Sticks And Stones

These twists and turns of fate

Time falls away

But these small hours

These small hours

Still remain

All of my regret

Will wash away somehow

But I cannot forget

The way I feel right now

In these small hours

These little wonders

These twists and turns of fate

Yeah, these twists and turns of fate

Time falls away

Yeah, but these small hours

And these small hours

Still remain

Yeah, oh, oh

Oh, they still remain

These little wonders

Oh, these twists and turns of fate

Georgia On My Mind

Time falls away

But these small hours

These little wonders

Still remain

"But blessed is the one who trusts in the Lord,

whose confidence is in him."

Jeremiah 17:7

The End – for now.

Printed in the USA
CPSIA information can be obtained
at www.ICGtesting.com
LVHW021546031024
792850LV00008B/245